T0146534

GOD
Will
Make
a Way

About the Author

Terry Rush is most qualified to write on the subject of pain and ultimate victory through his own personal experiences with pain. When his daughter's fiancé and his brother were brutally murdered by unknown assailants, Terry's world was shaken to its very core. His struggle to survive this ordeal and the lessons he learned through it will give you strength, comfort, and hope.

Terry has preached for the Memorial Drive Church of Christ since 1977. He has authored several books, including *The Holy Spirit Makes No Earthly Sense* and *Afraid God Works, Afraid He doesn't* and has produced a video interviewing several celebrities, *High Hope for the Human Heart.*

Twice a year Terry has been privileged to play baseball with former St. Louis Cardinals' players; this adventure has resulted in much teaching, counseling, and conversions. In 1992, Upper Deck Baseball Cards invited Terry to play baseball against former stars Reggie Jackson, Bob Gibson, Vida Blue, and others on the Field of Dreams in Dyersville, Iowa, where he was asked to deliver a special "Sermon on the Mound." Rush appeared on the November 1994 ESPN documentary "Dream Field" and shared how God fulfills the ultimate dream and how those attending the "Sermon on the Mound" responded to his preaching.

Terry and his wife, Mary, have three children: Wendy, Dusty, and Tim.

When there seems to be no way...

GOD Will Make a Way

TERRY RUSH

HOWARD
PUBLISHING CO.

3117 North 7th Street
West Monroe, LA 71291

Our purpose at Howard Publishing is:

- *Instructing* believers toward a deeper faith in Jesus
  Christ
- *Inspiring* holiness in the lives of believers
- *Instilling* hope in the hearts of struggling people
  everywhere

Because he's coming again

God Will Make a Way
© 1995 by Howard Publishing Co., Inc.
All rights reserved
Printed in the United States of America
Fourth printing 2002

Howard Publishing Co., Inc.,
3117 North 7th Street, West Monroe, LA 71291-2227

Cover Design by LinDee Loveland

ISBN 978-1-5822-9302-8

Scripture quotations not otherwise marked are from the New American Standard Bible.

With Fond Memory

Susan Martin
Bobby Phillips
David Phillips

This book is dedicated to these three. Each died suddenly in December 1992. Lovely, dark-eyed Susan was a living angel. She accomplished so much without any noise. Bobby was going to marry my "Wendy-the-Pooh." He gave everything early . . . including his life. David was God's own masterpiece. His goal was to work at Wal-Mart . . . so he could get to wear a tie.

We will always miss them.

C O N T E N T S

♦

ACKNOWLEDGMENTS

♦

A host of individuals gave me great input for the contents of *God Will Make a Way.* I want to thank my family, my friends, the staff I work with, and all at Howard Publishing. I am enthused about this work.

I mainly want to thank, genuinely and sincerely, the gracious Lord for guarding my heart from bitterness and for decorating my path with ornaments of hope while I moved along such a numbing corridor. The Father, Son, and Spirit hurried to help.

You will note many names throughout this book—all offered their personal touch of light that helped me find the end of the tunnel. This book would not carry its potent punch for recovery had these individuals not been willing to share their heartbreak.

Thank you, dear reader, for reading on when you'd find it easier to throw the book down, throw your hands up . . . and quit. You don't have to do any of that because . . . God will make a way.

Heartbreak

The invisible substance called meaning
had been drained from my life,
and most of what I saw now looked senseless:
the striving, the hopes, the dreams. The struggles.
Life didn't seem worthwhile.
Trying was stupid.
The force we were fighting felt overwhelming,
the odds not in our favor.

—Melody Beattie

♦

THE "OTHER PERSON" TURNED OUT TO BE ME

Tough stuff has always happened to the other person—some stranger in the newspaper or someone who lives two blocks over. But now it's you. You have felt so badly for others; who would ever believe this unbelievable event is yours?

Can anyone own anything this big? Does this really belong to you? Are you stuck with this? You didn't ask for this! Anger. Fear. Total shock. The unknown. The impossible. Is this a bad dream? It's much worse.

The hurt is so gigantic that you can't comprehend the depth of the wound. You need help. You need big help, and you know it. But how, what, where, when, and who? Un-answers keep trying to pull you under.

God Will Make a Way is a book with arms . . . arms to hold you. Let this book lead you to the arms of God. Let him caress you entirely. Be still. Let him guide; let him talk; let him listen; let him cry with you. All of your schemes have been dismantled. There seems to be no way. God will make a way.

I am grateful for my handicap,
    for through it I found my world,
    my self, and my God.

—Helen Keller

♦

ONE

MY STORY

The evening of December 7, 1992, best I recall, had a cool crisp edge in the air. Mary and I returned home from a Christmas play to find a note from our daughter, Wendy, that was not in the least bit alarming. "Have gone with Mark McCoy. Will call you later." Simple enough.

Little did we know that backing those two simple sentences was the unleashing of hellish terror and pain. Just moments later the phone rang. Its message, now months later, is still all too clear.

In a very deliberate voice, our dear neighbor, Judy McCoy, carefully spaced each word. "Terry-I'm-so-sorry-to-tell-you-this—Something-terrible-has-happened—Wendy's boyfriend-has-been-killed—And-Terry-it-wasn't-an-accident—It-looks-like-someone-has-murdered-him-and-his-brother—Mark-has-taken-Wendy-to-the-scene—I-am-so-sorry-to-have-to-tell-you-this-Terry—I-am-so-sorry—."

I thanked her the best I could, and in shock, hung up.

Although I remained standing, I couldn't verify that there was a floor beneath me. I picked up where Judy's cadence left off and repeated the message to Mary. This information was too stunning to be heard, let alone be true.

I just stood. My first thought was, "God, how would you think I ought to handle this?" It was too hard to hear. I had to call Judy back and ask her to repeat everything she had just said to be certain I had heard her right.

Twenty-six year old Bobby Phillips was engaged to Wendy. He had called from work that evening and was to be at our house by seven. But first, he had to run home to change clothes.

Although I had heard Judy twice, I still thought she must have had the story wrong. Most likely the boys had been badly hurt . . . but not killed. I was pretty sure someone had gotten a little overanxious and had exaggerated parts of the story.

Mary and I headed immediately for Bobby's house. The night air had turned soupy with fog. The speedometer read 55 mph. But it seemed the car was moving so much slower. My hips and legs didn't have any feeling.

Neither of us said much in the car. One would mumble something about Wendy. Much later another would ask what the possibility was that someone had simply misunderstood. Maybe it wasn't a murder, but rather an accident. Maybe he wasn't dead. Not Bobby.

I didn't think we would ever get to his house. On the other hand, I didn't want to get there.

We wove through the heavy fog that lulled the streets into quiet slumber. The closer we got, the more anxious we became. Shock seemed to make everything too strange. My whole being felt as out of place as an arm that goes to sleep in the middle of the night. This was all too wrong.

It was a strain to read the street signs. As we found the entrance to their housing addition, an ambulance was leaving. We moaned. Shortly, we came around a corner, and the fog was pierced by a staggering scene.

Squad cars with their kaleidoscopic flashing lights were everywhere. Yellow tape rudely barricaded the Phillips' lawn and house against the rest of the neighborhood. Enormous gigantic sickness rushed in and drowned my heart. It was true.

Light beamed from every room of the house. The roof line and shrubbery were dancing with strings of Christmas lights. The house itself spoke of irony. Something was brightly wrong.

Reporters moved about doing their job. Television crews, along with trucks and equipment, added to the overwhelming assurance that Judy's words were, after all, true.

We approached a neighboring house that was being used as "police headquarters." I really preferred not to step through the door. We entered into massive heartbreak. Bobby's parents, Wanda and Bob, sat on a sofa. Wanda sat with her arm around Bob, who was slumped in tears. His jacket was stained with Bobby's blood. A police chaplain somewhat anchored the room while the policemen and policewomen continually moved back and forth between this house and the Phillips'.

Enormous, gigantic sickness rushed in and drowned my heart. It was true . . .

I found Wendy in the next room with Mark McCoy. She was white. Her countenance was totally blank. Her heart was blown away. Her fiancé was dead. Words were futile; their combinations did little to mend the moment. Hugs, tears, broken sentences, and a lot of coffee filled the hours ahead.

Intermittent sobbing verified that the night was filled with grievous disorientation. In and out. . . . in and out—the detectives were hustling. The woman whose home we were using ministered sweetly to us: "The phone is clear now. Would anyone care for more coffee?"

10

Mary stayed with Wendy. I moved from Wendy, to Bob and Wanda, to the phone, and then circled again . . . and again. I called my boys and told them what I couldn't bear for them to hear. Mostly, I sat with Wendy on the floor against an out-of-the-way bare wall. Maryann and Brad (Bobby's sister and her husband) came in from an otherwise enjoyable evening to be pelted with the worst. It was unbearable to watch this evening unfurl its nightmarish saga.

Police worked in overdrive, while the rest of us sat with glazed eyes and did our best to think of something intelligent to say. I heard one officer ask Bob and Wanda if they owned an ax. What in the world had happened to our boy?

The events of the double murder remain sketchy. Bobby's nineteen-year-old brother, David, had been home alone. David was mentally handicapped. At approximately 5:00 p.m. someone had entered the house, had shot David in the head, and had then strangled him. It is possible that when Bobby came home, he noticed that something was dangerously wrong.

It appears that he entered from the garage into the kitchen, picking up an ax along the way. The intruder(s) turned the weapon on him and also stabbed him. This clean-cut, handsome, hardworking boy was ruthlessly bludgeoned to his death.

The next few days were treacherous. At night, wails muffled by her pillow could be heard coming from Wendy's room. Sometimes there would be a shift into perpetual sobbing. Her terrifying nightmares would awaken us all.

11

Our world of friends overwhelmed us with warmth, compassion, and love. The Phillipses, too, were bombarded with consoling strength from those who loved them. The grief was suffocating all the while. It killed me to know why people constantly brought food to the house. Flowers were everywhere . . . absolutely everywhere.

Television reporters repeatedly came to our home for interviews. Other media would call wanting to know the floor plans to the Phillips' house, etc. I believe the worst experience of my life was when I took Wendy to the funeral home. Due to the blows to Bobby's head, whether the family should view his body was undecided. A couple of his cousins and I went in first to determine if others should follow. Viewing was permitted.

The right side of the skull had received extensive trauma. Wendy continually patted his face and felt his arms and chest. Suddenly she said, "Daddy, look at this over here." She was pointing to the undamaged left side of his head and face. "Look how smooth it is over here. Could we turn him around?"

It took a lot of explaining to convince her that we could not. With a certain peace, she sighed, "Oh well, I'm just going to always remember the good side."

December 11 presented a picture too baffling. The pace of pain seemed to gain speed and weight. Tom Bedicek, the minister of Bob and Wanda's church, opened the services of the double funeral. Mitch Wilburn, David's youth minister, spoke in honor of David. I was privileged to preach the funeral of Bobby, who had become my own son.

To look into the eyes of family and friends was incomprehensible. We three men didn't have the strength to carry this load. There was an unspoken respect for each other's brokenness. It was only and literally by the genuine assistance of God that we functioned. Each was conscious, and that was the extent of our strength for the moment.

Once again, there was no feeling in my hips or legs. Unsure whether I was making contact with the floor, I felt a floating sensation. I kept feeling as if I might collapse and feared that Tom and Mitch would be forced to hold me up while I addressed those packed into the church building.

The days following were streams of bewilderment. Numbness sometimes showed signs of dissipating. I felt extremely close to God. He was doing the work for I was far too weak to function. The Lord was always strong; I never was. Sorrow flooded my mind, heart, and soul.

Chaos ensued. Detectives warned the Phillipses and us that additional lives might be at risk. Guard dogs were brought into both homes. For days, the local news interviewed Bobby and David's family and Wendy and myself. For weeks after the incident, it was not unusual to hear the radio announcer say: "The latest on the murder of Bobby and David Phillips . . ." Sometimes I could take it.

When I came home in the evenings, I would often find Mary sitting in the dark, replaying the events in her mind. Sometimes I would find Wendy folded in tears on her bed. But even so, only moments later, Wendy would say something that would let me know she was going to come through this. We were always aware that Bob, Wanda, Maryann, and Brad were across town, also feeling stunned and hurt. Everyday I expected to be done crying. I did well in front of people . . . sometimes. I cried the hardest and the hottest and the longest in the shower. I felt like something must be wrong with me, that I shouldn't be this devastated. I finally had to quit telling myself that I wouldn't cry anymore. I still cry.

I don't know what others thought of how we were doing. I don't know how we ought to have done. God was doing good in us, though.

Thirteen days from the funeral, pain increased its pace. Friends of ours, Chris and Linda Jones had gone with Mary and me to the Christmas play the night the boys died. Linda's sister, Susan Martin, was also a dear friend.

I finally had to quit telling myself that I wouldn't cry anymore. I still cry.

During the week before Christmas, Linda commented several times that Susie was not feeling well. She seemed to have come down with the flu, which was certainly an inconvenience while trying to get details for the big holiday in order. She finally became so ill that she called for her mother, Linda Myers, to come to help.

Before long, Chris and Linda were called to the city. Susan had been hospitalized, and it appeared somewhat serious. I called the Martin's house about five that evening. Chris said that David (Susan's husband), Linda, and her mother had just been called to the hospital. I called the waiting room. Linda was crying.

Treatment was ineffective. She asked me to call a Tulsa doctor friend of David's to see if he had any insight as to what could be done for her sister. Contact with Dr. Reese was immediate. Just as quickly (maybe three minutes), I returned a call to the waiting room to let Linda know of my conversation with Joe Reese. I asked the woman if I could speak to Linda Jones. The voice on the other end very carefully said, "I'm sorry, but Susan didn't make it." It was Christmas Eve.

I put my head on the table and sobbed away what was left of my heart. This just couldn't be happening. Mary, Wendy, and I cried; layers of grief were beginning to accumulate. I couldn't accept that now the Martins, Myerses (Susan's family), and Joneses were thrust into their own impossible swirling pit of disorientation. Not this. Not now. Not them.

David, Bobby and, now, Susie. This thirty-five year old wife and mother of three little boys had died of toxic shock syndrome as a result of infection in her hand. Susan Martin was perfect; she just was. And now she has disappeared. We hold her close in the wonders of memory.

A slight word revision of the late '60s song continually swept through my mind, "Have you seen Bobby, Martin, and David?"

This just couldn't be true. Mary and I drove immediately to Oklahoma City to be with this family

15

who hurt beyond measure. Everything becomes so foreign when we feel we have lost control. Individually, we find ourselves stripped of meaning.

I had conducted Bobby's funeral on December 11. I did Susie's on December 28. To watch the family file into the auditorium seemed all too impossible. Their facial expressions begged for someone to assure them that this was a mistake. How painful is pain! How unacceptable is this which we are forced to accept!

Was there a plug we could pull to make all of this stop? Did anyone know of a rewind button? How could this happen? This stuff happens to others, not us. None of us received any warning. There were no yellow lights of caution to prepare us for this unfathomable intersection.

"So, Terry, where was this God you say loves us? Where was his compassion? And of what benefit was your faith?" These haunting questions are the reason I reveal my story to you.

Early in December, a friend asked if I was working on a new book. I told him I was and that the theme was grief. He asked why I chose that topic. My only response, with a shrug of my shoulders, was that I felt from God that he was preparing me to write this book. Four days later the boys were murdered. Seventeen days after that, Susan passed away. And, here's the book.

I believe *God will make a way*. This book is intended to help individuals who can't do stress another moment. The remaining chapters will point depressed and discouraged souls to incredible hope in God. What I have endured, I can't fathom. What I

16

have experienced has been wonderfully privileged and blessed. I have tasted ruin. God has hurried to help. He has made a way when there seemed to be no way.

The events I share with you reveal multiple personal weaknesses found in me. I share my story that you may know the glory and beauty and power of God. The radiance of the diamond shows up best when placed against the darkest cloth.

I have eaten at the table of spiritual poverty that I might pass the plate of encouragement.

♦

Grief can't choke out our hope if God has our permission to spend that hope. Rather, grief gives way to delight and eventual joy. As Jack Hayford said in *Leadership* magazine,

> Trials cannot be avoided, but they can be navigated. Pain will come, but it will be healed in the presence of Jesus—maybe not overnight, but the healing will come.[1]

I can't say that we ever get over significant loss. By his work in us, though, we do get on. We move forward with great tears, assured healing, enormous sorrow, comfort from the Spirit, painful reminders, happy reminders, and hope. He alone will make a way.

In other words, when I write of the privilege and joys of pain and the ultimate hope and victory available, you will understand that I know grief from life—not from a textbook. I have sampled it firsthand so that I could know how you feel in your awful pain. I have eaten at the table of spiritual poverty that I might pass the plate of encouragement.

As you try to pick up the pieces, I give my support. When you stare off into endless space, I gaze there myself. When you talk of the deceased as if they were alive (having momentarily forgotten they are not), I have done the same. When your tears have nearly drowned you and your mind won't quit rehashing the series of events, I have communion with your pain.

Therefore, I insist . . . when there seems to be no way, God will make a way. Hope is on its way . . . from above!

GOD
Will
Make
a Way

Hope

I know this.
    You can't die from crying . . .
    . . . or I'd be dead.

—Paula D'Arcy

♦

T W O

SOMEDAY, I WILL
BE ME AGAIN

It has always happened to the other person. But now you are the victim. You have been thumped. And it takes your breath away. Hope illudes you. Confusion is everywhere.

Horrifying, stark blankness sits in the pit of your stomach. Your mind is empty. Nothing matters. Nothing registers. Nothing motivates.

Oh how I wish you hadn't encountered your mishap. How I wish you didn't have to go through one moment of this. But the frightening truth is that it has happened, and due to this present struggle, you may never be the same.

Things will never be the way they were. Tragedy has struck. You are severely wounded. Things will be better, or they will be worse; but they will not be restored to how they were. But I am here to tell you that you *can* be you again. You *can* carry on as a wounded survivor and face the days ahead with hope of recovery. God will make a way.

I am here to tell you that you can carry on as a wounded survivor and face the days ahead with hope of recovery.

Max Lucado, in *In the Eye of the Storm,* tells of one little fella's mighty rough day.

Chippie the parakeet never saw it coming. One second he was peacefully perched in his cage. The next he was sucked in, washed up, and blown over.

The problems began when Chippie's owner decided to clean Chippie's cage with a vacuum cleaner. She removed the attachment from the end of the hose and stuck it in the cage. The phone rang, and she turned to pick it up. She'd barely said "hello" when "sssopp!" Chippie got sucked in.

The bird owner gasped, put down the phone, turned off the vacuum and opened the bag. There was Chippie—still alive, but stunned.

Since the bird was covered with dust and soot, she grabbed him and raced to the bathroom, turned on the faucet, and held Chippie under the running water. Then, realizing that Chippie was soaked and shivering, she did what any compassionate bird owner would do . . . she reached for the hair dryer and blasted the pet with hot air.

Poor Chippie never knew what hit him.

A few days after the trauma, the reporter who'd initially written about the event contacted Chippie's owner to see how the bird was recovering. "Well," she replied, "Chippie doesn't sing much anymore—he just sits and stares."

It's hard not to see why. Sucked in, washed up, and blown over . . . that's enough to steal the song from the stoutest heart.[1]

And you? I'm confident a song has been stolen from your heart. Your days have taken on the beatings of Chippie's. Blow dryers are one thing. Blown hearts are another.

But you will recover.

> Do you not know? Have you not heard? The Everlasting God, the LORD, the Creator of the ends of the earth does not become weary or tired. His understanding is inscrutable. He gives strength to the weary, and to him who lacks might He increases power. Though youths grow weary and tired, and vigorous

young men stumble badly, yet those who wait for the LORD will gain new strength; they will mount up with wings like eagles, they will run and not get tired, they will walk and not become weary. (Isaiah 40:28–31)

This book is intended to give you genuine, tangible hope. Your hurt may be so heavy that the thought of recovery does not interest you. But you are stronger than you think. You have already crawled over hurdles that were impassable, as well as impossible. You will increase in that strength. Someday, you will be you again.

Your hurt may be so heavy that the thought of recovery does not interest you. But you are stronger than you think.

Read the following account of one woman's joy turned nightmare and her eventual victory. These excerpts come from the monthly journal of Paula D'Arcy, *Song for Sarah,*[2] and will warm your heart.

February 1973
Dear Unborn Child:
    Really, dear Andrew, (I'm sure you're an Andrew. And I am really, truly pregnant!) . . . I

don't know the words to express my heart's excitement.

May 1973
Dear Andrew:
    Why can't I look enormous? If you're there (and the doctor promises that you are) then I want to look full of you . . . I want to look positively pregnant. Poke out, why don't you?

June 1973
Dear Andrew:
    It's kinda scary, like tempting fate, but I bought you some clothes today. If I refold them and hold up each item one more time for your father's approval, they'll be worn out before you arrive. Everything is blue, so I hope you're you! . . . Then I sit and look at my belly. I love carrying you.

July 1973
Dear Andrew:
    This morning I patched your father's jeans. Then just you and I took such a long walk. We are so close. Your father says I'm an incurable romantic. Is that why I'm starting to cry about our shortly never being so close again? From the second you're born, you'll begin to pull away and start your own life. For just a little while longer it's us.

August 1973
Dear Andrew:
    How can I feel two opposites at once? I don't want this pregnancy ever to be over. I love

living near you. but when will it end? Haven't I been big-bellied forever?

October 1973
Dear Andrew:
    You're Sarah! I can't believe it! . . . The end was so fast—you insistent, me scared. And your daddy tripping to get into his delivery room "whites." And then you. Ten fingers, ten toes, little you. Perfect you.

November 1973
Dear Sarah:
    What's happening? Why are you crying? And why can't I figure out why you're crying? I thought I was as cool and capable as they came. But look at me. Who'd have guessed being a parent wasn't easy?
    In the hospital, motherhood all seemed adventurous and exciting. But here at home I'm way too tired to be poetic. Some days it's a contest to see who cries more, you or I.

January 1974
Dear Sarah:
    Was I really as harried as those thoughts I just re-read from November? It seems so much better now. I mean, I'm far from a pro, but I do think I'm getting used to us.

September 1974
Dear Sarah:
    How you love the cartoon segments! You delight in dancing in fantasy with Dancing Bear. You are so full of wonder at everything

new. And there will be a world to show you. It's
exciting.

August 1975
Dear Sarah:
   We were driving home from Grandma's. . . .
You squirmed. . . . I turned around to reach
your hand, all I knew was a white car driving at
us. My God.
   And now, just like nothing, just like the
earth, in a second, can be not the earth, they
are telling me, "I'm so sorry." I'm looking into
eyes full of pity and concern. I hear my voice
giving phone numbers, telling names, reassur-
ing strangers that I'm all right.

"Horror like this can't find room inside of me."

My act must be good. They whisper, "She's
so brave." My mouth goes right along. I tell
them not to worry about me . . . Roy and Sarah
are badly hurt. Roy and Sarah are dying.
   . . . This has to be a dream. How can I make
it a dream? Are you kidding? This can't be my
life. Make it go away. It's a joke. Horror like
this can't find room inside of me. I don't believe a thing.

Someday,

I Will

Be Me

Again

♦

August 1975
Dear Sarah:

I've stopped inside, but the outside of me refuses to recognize that everything has gone wrong. . . . they bring me three meals a day. They go on with their lives. They think the world is functioning. And I can't take charge to stop them. I can't even stop me. I'm lost to myself.

. . . It cannot get inside of me and become reality. I cry, but they are not my tears. I'm no longer me. I'm so far lost. How could this happen? Who can stop it? It has got to be stopped.

August 1975
Dear Sarah:

They said it's over. They said Sarah died this morning. What do they mean, "Sarah died this morning?" As if you were some separate person from me. You don't die. You just don't die without me dying too.

Your father will go crazy. He'll wake up from the coma and go crazy. We won't be able to go on. I cannot even believe that this is my life. It's like a play that won't leave, or stop.

August 1975
Dear Sarah:

I can't care. I can't care any more what they come in here and say. The feeling is gone. They've beaten me. They've won. They said that your father died. He's dead. Daddy's dead too. They have ripped my whole world. There is no more truth to come. They can't say anything else to me. Are they glad? Are they satisfied?

September 1975
Dear Sarah:
There are constantly people around and I
want to be alone. . . . Everybody said that I
couldn't stay there now. So I did what they said
to do. That's what I do now. But it's still awful
here . . . I was so good to you and I loved you
so. Why did you leave me?

September 1975
Dear Sarah:
I can't be polite to one more visitor. No one
would like me if they knew what I really was
thinking when they say how lucky I am that I
wasn't badly injured. That I lived.

"This new person doesn't have the energy left to do anything but stay alive and not scream."

. . . today I can't pass off the words. This
new person doesn't have the energy left to do
anything but stay alive and not scream. I don't
want to hear anyone else's awkward attempts.
They make me angrier than I already am.

September 1975
Dear Sarah:
I look at your clothes and your father's
clothes. It's all over now. The worries, the cares,

the events, the occasions. One day it all ends in clothes and shoes, deserted in a closet. They make the worries and ambitions seem so silly. They laugh out loud at everything superficial that we let matter. Because one day everyone's clothes will hang alone in their closet. And so what was it all for?

October 1975
Dear Sarah:
　. . . I cannot find me. I am a name from memory.

October 1975
Dear Sarah:
　Days and days and days go on. I'm here going through all the motions, but I'm not really here. I know I act almost right, but I'm not right. I'm not fooled at all.

November 1975
Dear Sarah:
　. . . What would our life be like today if you were both alive? What would we be busy with? Might I be sitting in our living room taking you both for granted, never guessing that this could happen?

December 1975
Dear Sarah:
　. . . I'm hanging on to sanity by a thread. My mind holds a madwoman who can't be shut off. I can't forget. I see people taking things for granted and I'm so angry with them without wanting to be.

. . . Am I any different? Did I ever value each day? Did I ever ask myself what in life had lasting meaning, and then live as though that mattered?

December 1975
Dear Sarah:
    I feel some rest. For a time I'm thinking about Mary and Bethlehem. I've lost all that I held most dear, and yet my life need not lose its meaning. Something says sorrow would have me were it not for Bethlehem.

"Something says sorrow would have me were it not for Bethlehem."

January 1976
Dear Sarah:
    . . . They no longer ask how I'm doing. They figure enough time has passed . . . and I don't blame them. I used to think grief went away quickly too.
    They try so hard to "involve" me again. . . . They look at my face and they assume it's me. They feel that I can do things again. They're ready for me to be well. But their conversation, their attempts, are all bouncing off this crazy mind. I'm not me. I'm cracking up.

February 1976
Dear Sarah:

. . . I may not be a madwoman. In fact, one day I could be me again. I know that right now that's just an idea. But it's such a strong, positive one.

. . . It's the strongest hope I've had. I might be me again!

. . . I think I dare to love again!

March 1976
Dear Sarah:

God did not finger you to die. Rather, nature had its way. Nature and man, neither perfect. But all of us are subject to the processes they set in motion. How guilty am I? What have my many thoughtless acts set in motion? How many times have I done nothing and so abetted the darkness? How responsible man is to this life.

"God changes neither the acts of nature nor of man. We remain free."

And God. Where is he? He changes neither the acts of nature nor of man. We remain free. He created us free, and with that terrible freedom we live. But the moment we prefer the Light, he transforms . . . he transforms not the circumstances, which we create—he transforms us. He transforms how we see what has been there all along. It never changes. We do.

March 1976
Dear Sarah:
Only today have I realized that I am not the only one who grieved. How could I not have known that? Our friends, our families—so many felt the loss. Your father's parents lost a child too. But it all escaped me. I have been so far away.

March 1976
Dear Sarah:
God, Love, did not move and does not change. So the question in life, every day, for every person, is not what can I enjoy, or who will I please, or how do I look, or what can I do or achieve. The question is, how do I love? Am I a channel for the Light?
I am sure of one thing, my little one. Emptiness is all around us. But if one chooses to look for God, he will not be empty and his life will never be the same. Christ has promised that. And no man avoids that choice, for to ignore it is to decide.

May 1976
Dear Sarah:
. . . But slowly my peace within grows. Can you understand that I still suffer over you and yet I am finding a way beyond it? There is pain and there may always be pain—but it no longer defeats me. I can go on. God's Light

transcends human suffering. The hope I cling to is strong and real.

July 1976
Dear Sarah:

I think I'm finally coming around. Somewhere in the near distance I see me.

August 1976
Dear Sarah:

I sat on my porch today feeling lonely. And as my mind wandered, I imagined that I had lived at the time of Christ. How lucky that would have been, I thought. Even loneliness would have seemed easier in his company.

And then it struck me and was so real: Christ does live, and we do live in the same time. No wishing and no "if only." Christ does live and his Love is here. He alone has never moved. That's the statement of the Resurrection. Nothing dies and nothing ends. When we reach one conclusion we only become part of another beginning. Your father wrote it in his Garden Log: "Every seed has its Easter." Now, finally, I understand.

January 1979
Dear Sarah:

I ached and sorrowed so at losing you. But the pain, in the end, did not have the final say. And so it was all much less a loss than a victory. For Love has the final say—"The Lord is my Shepherd, I shall not want." And we are all quite safe.

Paula's experience touches the entire scope of the pained heart—from the oblivious routine of the normal daily grind, to the shock of trauma, through the numbness of loss, into the rudeness of recovery, and finally to the conclusion of hope. She has been in your grave . . . and she made it. Her life today carries the torch of hope that God will make a way for you. And even though the Light has now transformed her, she still cries as she desperately misses Roy and Sarah.

Someday, I Will Be Me Again

♦

As was for Paula, it will be true for you: "One day I could be me again. I know that right now that's just an idea. But it's such a strong positive one."

One day you will be you again. One day you will sing again. Your song will be a new one, for you will have beheld new wonders that you would never have known otherwise.

Dull gravity cannot
   bind us to this earth,
   for heaven indwells us.
                    —Calvin Miller
                        ♦

THREE

SPIRITUAL ANSWERS FOR SPIRITUAL CREATURES

You were created by God. You are not mostly physical anymore than the surface of the earth is mostly land. It just looks that way because that is where you spend most of your time. You are a spiritual being, spirit driven. You have spirit receivers that tell you whether you are up or down, whether you are having a good day or bad.

Forearms, thighs, and spinal columns can't tell you how your day is going. Neither do they become enthused over a pay raise. Your spirit is at the center of everything because your spirit is the center of you. When the Creator speaks, you are wise to listen. As the student does not instruct the teacher, as the calf does not feed the cow, as the nest does not build the bird, so you must not attempt to advise God as to what is best for you. You must let him do his maintaining, providing, healing, sustaining, and guiding. You must trust him. Since he has brought you this far, you can be assured that he will carry you through. You can believe that he will make a way.

Therefore, what he says will work, will work. What he says will result, will result. What he says will help, will help. Why? He teaches the student, feeds the calf, and builds the nest. In other words, he has a feel for your life. As you look for answers, you must, therefore, look in the spiritual realm.

God's Way Is Not Your Way

From the start you must accept the truth that God's way of doing things is not your natural way. God is so unlike us, and yet we expect him to work in ways that make sense to us. This is why we so often lose our way. We look for answers that conform to our realm, forgetting that he works outside our boundaries and comprehension.

Brennan Manning, in the *Lion and Lamb*, reminds us that God is "Totally Other" than we.

> There is a chronic temptation to reduce God to human dimensions, to express Him in manageable ideas. Human reason seeks to under-

stand, to reduce everything to its own terms. But God is God. He is more than a super human being with an intellect keener than ours and capacity for loving greater than ours. He is Unique, Uncreated, Infinite, Totally Other than we are. He surpasses and transcends all human concepts, considerations, and expectations. He is beyond anything we can intellectualize or imagine. That is why God is a scandal to men and women—because He cannot be comprehended by a finite mind.[1]

Somehow, we must lay aside our human expectations so that we can see God's answers. Speaking of the disciples of Christ, Manning drives this point home:

> They looked for an unreal messiah of their own making and found a real one of God's making—but only after they were dispossessed of all the illusions and expectations. Expectations are our subtle attempts to control God and manipulate mystery. We can get so wrapped up in them that when Jesus breaks into our lives in new and surprising ways, we neither recognize Him nor hear His message.[2]

When you want to know the *hows* and *whys*, clear your mind of expectations and look up. And remember, when you receive the legitimate answer, it won't look like it. Too often we slay the hope we need with our unthought, "Yes, but . . . " And sometimes when solutions are given to us, we reject them because we had in mind something different, something easier. You are not shopping for new furniture.

39

You are trying to figure out how to make it through one of the roughest times you've ever encountered. You are not in the position to pick and choose answers. Your only hope lies in the Lord. Use the instrument he has placed in your hand. Do fishermen fish without a pole? Do mechanics repair without a wrench? Then why do we try mend our lives without the very instrument needed for our repair . . . the Spirit of our Lord?

Sometimes, we can learn from the mistakes of others. The ancient Israelites are an example of people who did not heed God's spiritual answers. While held hostage in Egypt, their freedom was shackled and they cried to the Lord for help. In response to their cry, the Lord sent Moses to rescue them. God displayed his magnificent power and love for his children by his fantastic parting of the Red Sea, and he promised them rich land coupled with a terrific lifestyle.

But the Israelites had a different sort of rescue in mind—an easier one. Instead of yielding to him and trusting him to bring them blessings, the freed ones murmured themselves to death. They committed a lengthy suicide by hanging themselves on the self-created gallows of stupid, faithless talk and constant whining. As a result, they griped themselves out of the blessing and into forty years of traipsing around in circles, going nowhere . . . but to their own deaths.

We have the opportunity to learn from their mistakes. In fact, 1 Corinthians 10:11 says that what happened to them was for our benefit. From their experiences we can learn that even when we don't understand God's ways, we can trust that he has our ultimate good in mind.

GOD'S WAY DOESN'T ALWAYS MAKE SENSE

Let me direct you to Isaiah 55. Here we see how nonsensical God's ways often appear to humankind.

> Ho! Every one who thirsts, come to the waters; and you who have no money come, buy and eat. Come, buy wine and milk without money and without cost. (v. 1)

Right away, we are struck with the unorthodoxy of God's offer. How can one who has no money buy and eat? He cannot, unless the Lord provides through means that cannot be fathomed by the natural mind.

> Why do you spend money for what is not bread, and your wages for what does not satisfy? Listen carefully to Me, and eat what is good, and delight yourself in abundance. (v. 2)

We, like the Israelites, run after answers that are really nonanswers. We chase after solutions that do not satisfy. But Jehovah calls us to what is truly "good." And even when you have nothing to offer in return, he supplies abundance. He calls your heart to new life . . . on his terms . . . and offers overflowing joy.

> Incline your ear and come to Me. Listen, that you may live; and I will make an everlasting covenant with you. (v. 3a)

41

Where is God when you need him? He is at your ear. He is begging you, the created one, to consider him, the Creator. And his only motive is that you might live.

> Behold, you will call a nation you do not know, and a nation which knows you not will run to you, because of the LORD your God, even the Holy One of Israel; for He has glorified you. (v. 5)

As God told the Israelites that their help would come from unknown nations (nations they didn't know and who didn't know them), so, too, your help will come from unexpected sources. It's like dialing for help without knowing the phone number, and help coming. When God makes a way, his answers will not come from the reserve of intelligent explanation.

Are you getting the message that God's ways are not our ways? Do not overlook his help. Seek him while you can.

> Seek the LORD while He may be found; call upon Him while He is near. (v. 6)

Oswald Chambers in *The Love of God,* reminds us that God's ways defy our "common-sense."

> "God was in Christ, reconciling the world unto himself" (2 Corinthians 5:19). These are subjects that have no weight with us in our ordinary way of looking at things. They do not live in the same street because they are not in the street, but in the foundations of things. When war or some other calamity hits us hard and

knocks us out of the commonplace, we are prepared to listen to what the Bible has to say, and we discover the Bible deals with the foundation of things that lie behind our common-sense life. The Bible does not deal with the domain of common-sense facts. We get at those by our senses. The Bible deals with the world of revelation facts, which we only get at by faith in God.[3]

Your Way Brings Misery

I guarantee you that if you opt to go your own way, you will be miserable. Not because I know you personally, but because I know that if it is not his way, it will not pan out. Our inventive processes are nothing but fools' gold.

To test your way, ask yourself these questions: How am I doing with my alternative plan, with my idea of how it ought to go? Am I happy? Content? At peace?

If you follow God's way, you may still shed tears, but your lips will speak words of hope. If it is your way, you will shed tears while your speech meanders in circles of bewilderment.

Choose to depend on him and his backward ways.

The Choice Is Yours

It's true. Your invisible spirit is visibly shaken. You are in ruin. But you are not without choice. In fact, you have more control over the situation than you might imagine. While you do not have the choice to turn back the clock and restore things to their original order, you do have the choice of going under or going up! Which will it be? It's up to you.

Every situation, every pain, can go one of two ways: it can depress or motivate. It's up to you.

Have you ever noticed that two people with similar problems can have opposite characters? One whines. The other praises. One is never well. The other, though ill, accents the good days. Why? Because some actually fall into the trap of worshiping pain and unhappiness. They are ruled by these phony gods . . . because they choose to be. Others have exhausted themselves of self and have learned to depend on God for solutions. Every situation, every pain, can go one of two ways: it can depress or motivate. It's up to you. In the midst of your pain, you can give up on God, or you can find him. The choice is yours.

When you encounter tragedy, you have two choices: (1) to go insane and spend your remaining days saturated in grief—blaming God, blaming others, and blaming self. Or, (2) to go to school and learn from the hurt. What you learn in the school of pain will find purpose in helping others who hurt.

If you so choose, you can read the map and un-
cover the treasure. It's not luck, not a break, but a
choice. You can depend on God and look for his unfathomable riches, or you can dig for the dirty, the
disgusting, and the damnable. You will find the very
thing for which you dig. You can trust God or you
can try to solve it yourself. The former will bring you
joy. The latter will leave you withered, ruined, and
very old. Either is guaranteed. You choose.

Two factors are always present in your life: Satan
with his evil and the Lord with his help. (Note that
evil is the backward spelling of live.) You have no
choice as to whether you will struggle, agonize, or
hurt. But you can choose your reaction. Don't try to
change the things you can't. Work on those you can.
The tried and proved words of the Serenity Prayer,
by Reinhold Niebuhr, still offer sound direction for
you today:

God grant me the serenity to accept
the things I cannot change;
Courage to change the things I can,
and the wisdom to know the difference.

God extends his help to you. You can choose to
accept his offer. You can anticipate that he will come
through for you. You can plan to be all right. You can
intend to let the heavenly Father handle your private
situation with great class. The choice is yours.

If God did not have nail-pierced hands,
I would not be interested in Him;
a God who doesn't care, doesn't count.

—E. Stanley Jones

♦

GOD CARES

If you are attempting to follow the advice of the last chapter—to look to God for spiritual answers—then the first thing you need to know as you look to him is that *he cares*. He has not abandoned you. He is right beside you and has been there all along.

The Bible assures us that God is near and that he loves us.

> The LORD is righteous in all His ways, and kind in all His deeds. The LORD is near to all who call upon Him. (Psalm 145:17–18a)

47

The Old Testament prophet, Jeremiah, echoes our despair and heralds our hope:

> My eyes pour down unceasingly, without stopping, until the LORD looks down and sees from Heaven. . . . I called on Thy name, O LORD, out of the lowest pit. Thou hast heard my voice, "Do not hide Thine ear from my prayer for relief, from my cry for help." Thou didst draw near when I called on Thee; Thou didst say, "Do not fear!" (Lamentations 3:49–50, 55–57)

He hears your sobs and he sees your tears. He is compassionately aware when you break down over that slight thing that reminded you of your pain. He measures your pit. You are not out of his reach. He—not you and not me—will set your feet on solid ground.

God does not minimize your pain.

God does not minimize your pain. He is fully aware that you face difficulty everyday. Notice the often overlooked last sentence in Matthew 6:34:

> Therefore do not be anxious for tomorrow; for tomorrow will care for itself. Each day has enough trouble of its own.

The statement in the last sentence assures you that God is not numb to your pain. If he had said, "You think *that* is a problem? You don't know what true problems are. You think *you* are suffering pain? Let me tell you about real pain," then you would have reason to feel abandoned. But such is not his approach.

The Lord never addresses you in such a manner. Why? He knows this stuff is hard for you. He knows because he sent Jesus to interpret human hurt. He sampled it. The report Jesus filed in heaven was, "It's difficult—at times beyond bearing." God does not advise, "Do not regard as difficult," but rather, "Do not be anxious." The Lord is not in denial. Neither does he expect you to be.

♦

He Has Been There . . . Ahead of You

In the midst of crisis, your mind floods with questions. Does God care? Where was he when I needed him? What has he done to help me in my personal trial? Frustration builds. But, be encouraged. Not only is God aware, he has been there in the depths of your ruin . . . ahead of time. He has worked to make a way.

Does God care? God demonstrates his love for you in that he allowed Jesus to know your pain. Jesus' experience on the cross put him in the center of your crisis—tasting it, wearing it, measuring it, enduring it, dying with you over it . . . ahead of time . . . at Calvary.

Where was God when you needed him? Centuries earlier, he was carrying out the plans to deal with your specific crisis—plans that would provide avenues for your survival. God was working on your case before your nightmare began.

What did God do for your personal trial? He walked in your shoes before you had feet. He knows your shoe size. He was there to presuffer your pain in order to know exactly how to pay the bill . . . your bill. Not only has he provided heaven in the long run, he offers hope for the present.

Your divorce, your tumor, your depression, your loss, your disappointment, your greatest fear—all had his undivided attention . . . before you experienced them. Before you hit your crisis, he was there like an insurance adjuster estimating the damage, weighing your needs, preparing your solution. He is even now waiting for you at your next tragedy and your next one.

God makes a way when there seems to be no way.

He is not the Red Cross that comes to the site of the disaster after it occurs. He comes from *the* cross; he is not only there before you arrive at the scene, he is there ahead of the scene. Referring to the intense attention of our invisible Father, David Redding said,

> Before God ever created earth, and risked the cry that came from there, He had already determined that He could handle it. That cross would not be too big for Him to carry, nor the stone too large to roll away. He knew all along, as Christ sweat through Gethsemane and struggled up that last hill, that He would surely rise again; and when He repeated, "Let there be light," this time there would be light the darkness could not overcome. God had the answer long before Adam and Eve bothered about the apple.[1]

He Suffered Like You

The ultimate testimony to God's care for you is seen in the sacrifice of his own son—his only son. God allowed Jesus to leave heaven so that you could have life. He allowed Jesus to suffer agony that you could know peace with him. God is not immune to your pain because he has suffered severe pain of his own.

Two thousand years ago, God oversaw the murder scene of his precious son. He agonized over the pain his son suffered so that he might ultimately remove your pain. Furthermore, in Jesus, God was on that beam of splinters and knots, paying the unbearable price in outrageous infliction that you could have hope when you struggle. He has not forsaken you.

♦

You will make it because Jesus paid the ultimate price for you. He was executed when he was only thirty-three. He encountered supreme disappointment, heart-breaking betrayal, terrorizing abuse, and death.

In the end, Jesus' best friend denied that he even knew him . . . repeatedly . . . publicly. On the night he most needed encouragement, his three closest friends couldn't stay awake to provide the slightest sign of support. The crooked court system did him in. Delivered to the cross, the physical anguish of muscle spasms alone were torturous and excruciating.

In addition to all of this, God, through his son, underwent loneliness, agony, screaming, crying, confusion, darkness, disillusionment, and frustration. Do these emotions sound familiar to you? They are exactly the emotions you feel! In other words, the

Lord went to bat for you. He did not carry a poster in your support; he lay in a grave . . . dead . . . to demonstrate his concern for you and me.

He did not carry a poster in your support; he lay in a grave to demonstrate his concern for you and me.

Why did Jesus leave heaven and suffer the agonies of being a man? Because he wanted to be able to say with authority, "I understand. I definitely know how you feel." The Hebrew writer increases our faith with these words of comfort,

> Since the children share in flesh and blood, He Himself likewise also partook of the same, that through death He might render powerless him who had the power of death, that is, the devil; and might deliver those who through fear of death were subject to slavery all their lives. For assuredly He does not give help to angels, but He gives help to the seed of Abraham. Therefore, He had to be made like His brethren in all things, that He might become a merciful and faithful high priest in things pertaining to God, to make propitiation for the sins of the people. For since He Himself was tempted in that which He has suffered, He is able to come to the aid of those who are tempted. (Hebrews 2:14–18)

Did you catch the comfort? He was "made like His brethren in all things, that He might become a merciful and faithful high priest." He is sympathetic because he has been there.

> Since then we have a great high priest who has passed through the heavens, Jesus the Son of God, let us hold fast our confession. For we do not have a high priest who cannot sympathize with our weaknesses, but one who has been tempted in all things as we are, yet without sin. Let us therefore draw near with confidence to the throne of grace, that we may receive mercy and may find grace to help in time of need. (Hebrews 4:14–16)

♦

Every emotion you go through, he also experienced. His struggle was not random. It had purpose. Not only did God create you, he underwent your entire range of feelings. He test drove your life in the man named Jesus.

He Defeated Satan for You

Satan wants you to believe that all hell has broken loose. He wants you to believe you have no hope. But the truth is that although Satan meant this tragedy for evil, all heaven is breaking loose to come to your aid.

Remember that God literally went through hell for you. He did not intend for murder and wars and hunger and disease and mental torture to exist. When Satan stained creation in the Garden, your creator took immediate action.

With intensity and in a hurry, the Lord was upon the scene of devastation in the Garden. Adam and Eve had eaten the forbidden fruit. Sin had now ruined the new creation. And God? He responded to the situation with this:

> I will put enmity between you and the woman, and between your seed and her seed; He shall bruise you on the head and you shall bruise him on the heel. (Genesis 3:15)

Although Satan meant this tragedy for evil, all heaven is breaking loose to come to your aid.

This response says that he was at work for you before you were. It says that Satan will bruise the heel of Jesus by temporarily killing him, but that the Son will deliver the death blow to Satan.

He Is Able

Three great words for your circumstance today are "He is able." How profound! How significant! He is able to help us because he, too, has gone through the hurt. Remember that Hebrews 2:18 said, "He Himself was tempted in that which He has suffered." He did it! He made a way!

God is neither handicapped nor weary in the midst of your pain. His strength will deliver you—not barely, but mightily. Have you ever noticed that in the midst of trauma God never expresses confusion nor is he baffled as to what to do? He is not like "the king's horses and the king's men" who did their best to put Humpty-Dumpty together again. Rather, he *knows* how to hold you together. Your life is under control, even though you may think the wheels are falling off.

God is our refuge and strength, a very present help in trouble. Therefore we will not fear, though the earth should change, and though the mountains slip into the heart of the sea; though its waters roar and foam, though the mountains quake at its swelling pride. (Psalm 46:1–3)

He Fills You with Confidence

It is amazing that you have gotten through any of your personal ordeal. You have gotten this far because God was on the scene in a hurry. You can count on him. You will be all right. While you wrestle and experience moments of healing, you have my genuine sympathy, but be assured that God hurries to help.

His sympathy plus your devastation equals confidence in his most definite help. Your increasing awareness of God will not, at first, necessarily make your troubles any less difficult. What it will do is begin to offer some semblance of security and confidence that you have not been abandoned by the living Lord.

Be confident that God hurries to help. This hurrying to the scene is captured in the story of the prodigal son. The father raced to the dispirited and downtrodden child, and he restored the injured child, even though the child had rebelled and brought misery on himself. Only God loves this way.

God hurries to bless. Ask Wanda, ask Wendy, ask Linda if they did not see God's grace flickering among the ruin and rubble of shock.

May he hurry to bless.

GOD
Will
Make
a Way

Pain's Joy

It was only when I lay there
        on rotting prison straw
        that I sensed within myself
the first stirrings of good.

Gradually, it was disclosed to me
        that the line separating good and evil passes,
                not through states,
                nor between classes,
                nor between political parties either,
but right through all human hearts.

So, bless you, prison,
        for having been in my life.
                                —Alexander Solzhenitsyn

                                ♦

THE PRIVILEGE
OF PAIN

In the midst of your pain, I say with certainty in the Lord—you are experiencing a privileged time. "How can you dare say that?" you cry. Read on, friend, and you'll see.

Dallas Willard wrote, "The greatest danger to the Christian today is that of pitching its message too low." [1] And I was tempted to pitch *this* message too low. Being aware of how numb you may be, it is difficult for me to approach you in your anguish and have the nerve to tell you that something good is going on. But I say it again—you are experiencing the privilege of pain.

The Prevalence of Pain

Before I explain your privilege, let's consider the prevalence and power of pain.

Pain is waiting at every intersection. It can multiply on you. It is abundant. Those who live without the Living God have no hope. C. S. Lewis was nakedly honest about pain when he wrote,

> The creatures cause pain by being born, and live by inflicting pain, and in pain they mostly die. In the most complex of all the creatures, Man, yet another quality appears, which we call reason, whereby he is enabled to foresee his own pain which henceforth is preceded with acute mental suffering, and to foresee his own death while keenly desiring permanence. It also enables men by a hundred ingenious contrivances to inflict a great deal more pain than they otherwise could have done on one another and on the irrational creatures. This power they have exploited to the full. Their history is largely a record of crime, war, disease, and terror, with just sufficient happiness interposed to give them, while it lasts, an agonised apprehension of loving it, and, when it is lost, the poignant misery of remembering. Every now and then they improve their condition a little and what we call civilisation appears. But all civilisations pass away and, even while they

remain, inflict peculiar sufferings of their own probably sufficient to outweigh what alleviations they may have brought to the normal pains of man.[2]

Life is full of pain. Even though we don't want to die and will fight to live, life is simply too rude. Every second of every day, messages flood the phone cables with news too baffling to hear. Our ears can scarcely translate.

Unless you learn how to deal with it, pain will become your slavemaster, driving you to a crippled life. My desire is to help you break the approaching paralysis that imposes restraint on your hopes and dreams.

Paul Brand and Philip Yancey wrote of the power of pain in their book, *Pain: The Gift Nobody Wants*.

All these characteristics of pain serve its ultimate end; to galvanize the entire body. Pain shrinks time to the present moment. There is no need for the sensation to linger once the danger remains. What matters to the pain system is that you feel miserable enough to stop whatever you're doing and pay attention right now.

In the words of Elaine Scarry, pain "unmakes a person's world." Try carrying on a casual conversation with a woman in the final stages of childbirth, she suggests. Pain can overrule the values we cherish most, a fact which torturers know all too well; they use physical pain to wrench from a person information which a moment before he had held precious or even sacred. Few can transcend the urgency of physical pain—and that is its intent, precisely.[3]

The Privilege of Pain

Without exception, every individual encounters noticeable stress. While its dosage varies from person to person and situation to situation, we all deal with it. What you need to know is that distress, pressure, and difficulty have *value*. Such value, though, is usually hidden. You must decide to find it.

"So Terry, if this is true, tell me the blessing in my house burning or my car crashing or, even worse, my son dying. Are you saying there is value in this?" This is where it gets tough. But this is the question to be addressed.

The answer is this: pain's privilege is found in its purifying process.

Pain's privilege is found in its purifying process.

⌒

Everyone who has experienced tragedy knows its ability to burn away the trivia in our lives. Regarding the purifying of our faith, read the inspired words of Peter.

> In this you greatly rejoice, even though now for a little while, if necessary, you have been distressed by various trials, that the proof of your faith, being more precious than gold which is

62

perishable, even though tested by fire, may be found to result in praise and glory and honor at the revelation of Jesus Christ. (1 Peter 1:6, 7)

Just as gold is purified through repeated encounters with fire, so are you. In the midst of your fire, you need to know you will live. "Terry, do you mean that your daughter is happier now that Bobby was murdered?" No. A year and a half into this and it is still so hard for her. It is hard for his parents, his sister, and his brother-in-law.

Yet, Wendy is stronger. Life works this way. Loneliness hurts her. The counseling sessions made her cry. All of it still makes me cry. Yet, the pain results in purification. Just as the dross and the gold are separated during the heating process, so our lives are clarified through the fires of pain.

God Knows What He's Doing

Charles Swindoll, in his book *Encourage Me,* makes the following observation:

> Heartaches and disappointments are like the hammer, the file, and the furnace. They come in all shapes and sizes: an unfulfilled romance, a lingering illness, an untimely death, an unachieved goal in life, a broken home or marriage, a severed friendship, a wayward and rebellious child, a personal medical report that advises "immediate surgery," a failing grade at school, a depression that simply won't go away, a habit you can't seem to break. Sometimes heartaches come suddenly . . .

other times they appear over the passing of many months, slowly as erosion of earth.

Do I write to a "nail" that has begun to resent the blows of the hammer? Are you at the brink of despair, thinking that you cannot bear another day of heartache? Is that what's gotten you down?

As difficult as it may be for you to believe this today, the Master knows what He's doing. Your Savior knows your breaking point. The bruising and crushing and melting process is designed to reshape you, *not ruin you*. Your value is increasing the longer He lingers over you.[4]

Joe Beam tells of the early years in the life of his retarded daughter Angela. Because of several birth defects, Angela had to be given medical tests in order that she be healthier. The tests hurt her badly.

Angela was physically very strong. Since the tests could not be administered with anesthesia, the doctors and nurses had a hard time holding her down. So the job of holding her head always fell to her daddy. And though she could not speak, Joe said that her eyes, in pain, would look at him and say, "You are my dad. Why are you letting them hurt me like this?"

What Angela didn't understand is what you and I so often don't understand. God lets us go through tests and trials in order that we might be stronger and healthier. Such is always the result when we eventually reach the proper conclusion.

F. B. Meyer teaches us about this process:

A friend of mine, spending a few days in the neighbourhood of our English lakes, came upon the most beautiful shrubs he had ever seen. Arrested by their extraordinary luxuriance, he inquired the cause; and learnt that it was due to a judicious system of transplanting, constantly pursued. Whatever may be the effect of such a process in nature, it is certainly true that our heavenly Father employs similar methods to secure the highest results in us. He is constantly transplanting us. And though these changes threaten at times to hinder all steady progress in the Divine life, yet, if they are rightly borne, they result in the most exquisite manifestations of Christian character and experience.

Another illustration of the same truth is given by the prophet Jeremiah, when he says, "Moab hath been at ease from his youth; and he hath settled on his lees; and hath not been emptied from vessel to vessel; neither hath he gone into captivity: therefore his taste remained in him, and his scent is not changed" (Jer. xlviii. 11). Grape juice, when first expressed from its ruddy chalice, is impure and thick; it is left in vessels for a time till fermentation has done its work, and a thick sediment, called lees, has been precipitated to the bottom. When this is done, the liquid is carefully drawn off into another vessel, so that all the precipitated sediment is left behind. This emptying process is repeated again and again, till the offensive odour that came from the "must" has passed away, and the liquid has become clear and beautiful. In the case of Moab, there had been none of this unsettling process; "he had not been emptied from vessel to vessel," and in consequence the people had made no moral or spiritual progress; "his taste remained in him and his scent was not changed." The quiet life is by no means the greatest life. Some characters can only reach the highest standard of spirituality by the disturbings or displacings in the order of God's providence.[5]

Helen Steiner Rice offers additional insight in one of her works:

> Our Father knows what's best for us,
> So why should we complain—
> We always want the sunshine,
> But He knows there must be rain—
> We love the sound of laughter
> And the merriment of cheer,
> But our hearts would lose their tenderness
> If we never shed a tear . . .
> Our father tests us often
> With suffering and with sorrow,
> He tests us, not to punish us,
> But to help us meet *tomorrow* . . .
> For growing trees are strengthened
> When they withstand the storm,
> And the sharp cut of the chisel
> Gives marble grace and form . . .
> God never hurts us needlessly,
> And He never wastes our pain
> For every loss He sends to us
> Is followed by rich gain . . .

And when we count the blessings
That God has so freely sent,
We will find no cause for murmuring
And no time to lament . . .
For our Father loves His children,
And to Him all things are plain,
So He never sends us *pleasure*
When the *soul's deep need is pain* . . .
So whenever we are troubled,
And when everything goes wrong,
It is just God working in us
To make *our Spirit strong*.[6]

The strong message of this poem may be hard to swallow in the midst of pain, but accepting this truth is vital to your progress. Thus, I'll not pitch this message too low. Through the tragedy you are experiencing, God is mysteriously working for your good. Since this dread is taking place and will not be undone, God will work in it for your progress.

The Blessing Is *in* the Pain

We tend to look for hope away from the pain and beyond the sorrow. This is precisely why our search for happiness or, at least relief, is so endlessly futile. We look in the wrong place. Rather than experience the blessing of manna in this bewilderness, we wander about in endless search for help.

It may be that what you are seeking is not true joy. You may simply be seeking freedom from suffering. If you seek God, you'll find him in the emergency room . . . blessing. Some who search for help from the Lord find that he is waiting with help in the very room they are so hurriedly trying to escape.

Of course you would rather not go through this. Of course you prefer not to suffer the loss. Of course. But that isn't your present reality. Something all wrong has happened to you. You cannot undo what has been done. If you could, you would.

As terrible tragedy strikes, you must believe that secrets to life are buried within, just waiting to be discovered. Remember that "in" all these things we overwhelmingly conquer (Romans 8:28). Good is found *in* devastation. I'm not merely talking about *surviving* pain, but actually finding enormous value in the center of pain. God will make a way.

> I'm not merely talking about *surviving* pain, but actually finding enormous value in the center of pain.

Only Christianity delivers victory in the center of the nightmare. The secret is this: you are being blessed now. After a while or beyond the turmoil is not the better times. It is "in all these things . . . " In. In. In.

When Susan, Bobby, and David died within days of each other, I had a choice to either go insane or go to school. By that, I mean that this trauma was so unmanageable that, if I had let it, it would have done me in. So I chose to learn what I could "in" the midst of it. As a result, my life did not diminish through digressive and obsessive self-pity. The reverse was true. I became advantaged for going through all of it.

When a bulb enters the ground to decay, a beautiful flower eventually blooms. Decay is a blessing. It is not merely a blessing to the beholder; it is a glory to the bulb itself. To remain a bulb without the pain of decay would be the greater sadness. It would have been spared the intimacy of destruction, remained intact, and lost all purpose.

The bulb is programmed to die in order to live . . . more gloriously. "For whoever wishes to save his life shall lose it, but whoever loses his life for My sake, he is the one who will save it" (Luke 9:24). So it is for each of us.

Consider the ultimate example of Jesus. His faith and dependence on God did not keep him out of the tomb. He died. Even those who find miraculous healing will eventually die. The victory is that he did not remain with his remains! In the midst of and in the center of the crucifixion, he had faith that he had already won! "Truly I say to you, today you shall be with Me in Paradise." Words of calmness in the midst of treacherous agony.

I ask you not to deny your deep pain. But be encouraged that while you are in the midst of dying over something dear to your heart, you are in the process of becoming greater, stronger, and more alive. You are not destined to spend your brief time upon this earth as a plain brown bulb. You are going to bloom!

Pain Is Necessary for Growth

Going through struggle and pain is necessary for growth. Students understand that the dreaded fungus called homework is necessary for learning. They regard it with disdain and displeasure; it is a burden. Its value is that through the difficulty of study the student grows. Who is stronger? The student who endures the study or the one who only eats, plays, and listens to the music? The one who endures will be better equipped to succeed. The one who avoids the work is in for major trouble because he won't accept the minor inconvenience set before him.

Brand and Yancey put it this way, "We silence pain when we should be straining our ears to hear it; we eat too fast and too much and take a seltzer; we work too long and too hard and take a tranquilizer."[7] Or as Augustine concluded, "Everywhere a greater joy is preceded by a greater suffering."

I not only deeply sympathize with you over your grief, I work to help you. I encourage you to enroll in the school of agony. I call you out of the prison cell of endless meandering in bewilderment to the land of the blessed and the territory of the healed.

There is hope in heartbreak . . . even in your heartbreak. God will make a way when you felt certain there would be no way.

What, then, are you supposed to learn from all you are going through? Good question. Great question. Here's the answer. Learn to depend on the Lord.

Helen Rice's poem, quoted earlier in this chapter, is correct, "He tests us, not to punish us, but to help us meet tomorrow." His ways are deep and rich.

Believe that blessings are not coming later, but right now in the very center of turmoil. Max Lucado wrote,

> I once heard that peace is not the absence of storms in our lives. Peace is what you get "in" the storm. Too many times I haven't allowed God to give me His peace in the storm because I was too busy trying to convince Him to get me out of there—post haste.[8]

Those things that hurt, instruct.

—Benjamin Franklin

◆

THE LESSONS
OF PAIN

Other than Valentine's Day, January and February can be pretty boring, even depressing for most of North America. Grass is brown and trees are bare. There are few signs of life. The first spring holiday is still ninety to one hundred twenty days away.

But the blah of January and February is a necessary prerequisite to the new beginnings of spring, the abundant growth of summer, and the eventual harvest of fall. Truly, all months are productive. Some months sow; others cultivate; others reap.

The first two of the productive twelve are not dead. During this time, the earth takes in nature's nutrients by resting. We may hate to see the fading of fall's beauty, but each hard winter day moves us closer to the tender warmth of spring. And, before we know it, we're marveling at fall again.

Right now, you may see no signs of green grass or budding trees. This may be your January/February of the human system. Don't let the appearance of non-productivity fool you. This dormant time is essential to your progress. September could not bring such a valiant harvest if the blank stress of January and February had not preceded it.

I want you to know that I am fiercely sympathetic toward you. Your hurt is not taken lightly. At one time, I could not have imagined what you are going through. Now I can.

From the time she turned eleven, Melody Beattie crossed off the days until she would turn eighteen and could leave the turmoil and pain of her family. Then, what she thought would be the marriage of her dreams ended in divorce. As a low-income, single parent, she was overwhelmed with trying to overcome poverty and loneliness.

> For the most part, life had been a series of disappointments. And the scale escalated as time went on. I could have what I wanted, but there would be a catch. Always. I was tired of the hooks, tired of the tricks, tired of watching life slip through my fingers as soon as I grabbed it.
> . . . The cold war turned white hot. I was in the ring with God. I wanted an explanation.

There didn't seem to be one. And, I wondered, how can you win a war with God?

Suddenly it hit her that she was experiencing these struggles for one reason . . . to learn to love. Forgiveness and faith and compassion and hope and joy—she was learning about all of these in this school for the spiritually blind.

> I saw now that even the struggles, the hard times when I cursed and moaned and whined, had not been punishment. God hadn't been peering down from the heavens saying, Good, let her crawl over broken glass for a bit. That will teach her. God was saying, Look she's learning to love.[1]

To some degree we all identify with Melody and her struggles. May we, too, feel connected to her valiant discovery. May we get it! May we catch on to the blessings in the center of our "dismayals." May we learn the lessons of pain.

Learn to Be Open to God's Way

Because of all you are going through, you are very possibly learning one major lesson already. Perhaps you are learning to consider the Lord's way. Why haven't you been open to it before? It might be that until now you have controlled everything. Perhaps you have been the provider and nourisher. But tragedy leads us to the blessed conclusion that we are helpless and dependent.

Your tragedy may seem bigger than life itself. But your ruin is not your demise. It is your opportunity to seek the Lord. It is your opportunity to learn that his ways are far different from yours.

> "For My thoughts are not your thoughts, neither are your ways My ways," declares the LORD. "For as the heavens are higher than the earth, so are My ways higher than your ways, and My thoughts than your thoughts." (Isaiah 55:8, 9)

His approach is so different. The world tells you that to get ahead you need to save and store. Yet, he says in order to receive we have to give it away.

> Give, and it will be given to you; good measure, pressed down, shaken together, running over, they will pour into your lap. For whatever measure you deal out to others, it will be dealt to you in return. (Luke 6:38)

The world tells you that life comes through preserving your health. Yet, he says that to live fully we need to die totally.

> He who has found his life shall lose it, and he who has lost his life for My sake shall find it. (Matthew 10:39)

You have heard it said that to be strong we need to build more stamina and muscle. Yet, he says that strength is found on an entirely different plane— that of weakness.

> My grace is sufficient for you, for power is perfected in weakness. (2 Corinthians 12:9)

His ways cannot be measured or sorted. Romans 11:33 is divinely breathtaking. "Oh, the depth of the riches both of the wisdom and knowledge of God! How unsearchable are His judgments and unfathomable His ways!" Get it into your thinking processes that you cannot fix everything. His way is true.

Way back in 1675, Michael Molinos penned this finely tuned insight:

> Perhaps you will come into darkness because you have had natural light removed from you. But remember that it may be in this darkness that you will first begin to find that supernatural light, within your spirit—a light which grows and increases in the midst of darkness! Often it is in times of dryness that wisdom and strong love are begotten.
>
> It is in times of darkness—not in times of great outward spiritual joy—that the self nature is dealt a mortal blow. Images, ideas, wanderings, and other hindrances—things which give you a distorted view of divinity—are consumed. Yes, it is by means such as those we have discussed here that the believer is led to the inward way.
>
> Last of all, the Lord uses these dry times to purge your outward senses; this purging is necessary for your internal progress.[2]

Learn That Brokenness Precedes Dependence

When you are finally broken of self-reliance, it is then that the floodgates of hope begin to open. Never before then.

> The sacrifices of God are a broken spirit; a broken and a contrite heart, O God, Thou will not despise. (Psalm 51:17)

> The LORD is near to the brokenhearted, and saves those who are crushed in spirit. Many are the afflictions of the righteous; but the LORD delivers him out of them all. (Psalm 34:18–19)

When you are finally broken of self-reliance, it is then that the floodgates of hope begin to open.

God even required that his own son be broken— "crushed" is the actual word used.

> But the LORD was pleased to crush Him, putting Him to grief; if He would render Himself as a guilt offering, He will see His offspring, He will prolong His days, and the good pleasure of the LORD will prosper in His hand. As a result of the anguish of His soul, He will see it and be satisfied (Isaiah 53:10, 11).

In your life, as in Jesus', brokenness brings spiritual prosperity. Why is it so important that you be broken? What's the big deal? The big deal is that you must learn to depend on God. Just as automobiles are not designed to drive themselves—as luxurious as they may be—you too must be guided by the driver who is behind the wheel. You were created/manufactured by God, and if you are to navigate through life properly, you must be led by him.

To be honest, I didn't know how to "do" murder. I'd never been around it. It still hurts so badly that my mind cannot grasp the stinging facts. How in the world could Susan go? No way! Exhausted of any form of helpful, personal contribution, I found myself at his mercy . . . broken.

As Betty Johnson, a friend whose mother was killed in a car accident, said, "You can hear about the need to be broken, but you won't know what brokenness is until you are broken. Then you will know it." Brokenness means that we break down. Pride and control break down and crumble, and we are left with our real selves. It is then that we are ready to listen, to depend on God.

Your heart may be broken, your eyes may be bleary, and your lungs may occasionally fight for air; but blessings will follow—for you have been wonderfully brought to the end of your own independence and forced to let God do for you what you could not do for yourself . . . he will make a way when there seems to be no way.

In *Heart Held High*, by Martha Snell Nicholson, we read these words:

We are now His broken things. But remember how He has used broken things; the broken pitchers of Gideon's little army, the broken roof through which the paralyzed man was lowered to be healed, the broken alabaster box which shed its fragrance abroad and the broken body of our Savior.

Let us ask Him to take our broken hearts and to press upon them further suffering to give us a poignant realization of the suffering of the world. Let us ask Him to show us the endless, hopeless river of lost souls. This will break our hearts anew; but when it happens, God can use us at last.[3]

Broken, dependent hearts are what God is after. Give him yours.

Learn What Is Truly Important

A portion of a quote from chapter 5 is worth repeating here:

Pain shrinks time to the present moment. . . . What matters to the pain system is that you feel miserable enough to stop whatever you're doing and pay attention *right now.*[4]

How true. Pain blesses us by shrinking time to the present moment. If pain's purpose is to get us to pay attention "right now," can't we see its advantage? When people are in crisis they often say things like, "Nothing else matters" or "This sure makes you realize what's important." How many times do we allow ourselves to become angry when the refrigerator bulb burns out or when someone butts in front of us at the supermarket. We go nuts over nothing! Yet, we can't see it until we are pained deeply.

Tragedy has a way of weeding out the silliness in us. It puts important matters into proper priority. Countless numbers will live forever in heaven because trauma awakened their senses to their own lack and led them to God.

Tragedy has a way of weeding out the silliness in us.

Learn That Your Pain Can Benefit Others

The words spoken by Joseph to his brothers can be spoken by us to Satan:

> And as for you, you meant evil against me, but God meant it for good in order to bring about this present result, to preserve many people alive. (Genesis 50:20)

Your suffering can be used by God "to preserve many people alive." The apostle Paul put it this way:

> Blessed be the God and Father of our Lord Jesus Christ, the Father of mercies and God of all comfort; who comforts us in all our affliction so that we may be able to comfort those who are in any affliction with the comfort with which we ourselves are comforted by God. . . .

But if we are afflicted, it is for your comfort and salvation; or if we are comforted, it is for your comfort, which is effective in the patient enduring of the same sufferings which we also suffer. (2 Corinthians 1:3–4, 6)

Sometimes you encounter rugged terrain in order to benefit someone else. The lessons and comfort you receive in your hardship can be passed on to others.

On the day of our family's disaster, Wendy was already talking of seeing amazing blessings from God. I didn't show them to her; God did. Because these three were swept from our midst so quickly, we saw people return to the Lord who had turned their backs on him years earlier. We saw relationships strengthened and/or established. We saw God bless churches. We saw media give such amazing and positive coverage regarding the victims and their families that it warmed the neighborhoods. We saw a sleepy city shaken for good regarding spiritual matters. We saw relatives refocus priorities. We saw friends find a way to make a difference by serving the Martins, Myerses, Phillipses, Joneses, and Rushes.

The lives of Susan, Bobby, and David did not end nor were their deaths wasted. These three have a story to tell . . . you. You are gaining significant strength and energy from their disasters.

Learn That Blessings Come from Tragedy

Wendy told me that the main thing she would want others to know is that blessings come out of tragedy. That statement comes from one who suffered excruciating pain.

Dr. Norman Vincent Peale, the father of "positive thinking," learned the blessings of tragedy firsthand when he and his wife were doggedly trying to get *Guideposts* off the ground.

> It was a shoestring operation at best. But it was an operation based on faith. . . . Friends took pity on the fledgling venture and tried to help. Lowell Thomas, a Pawling neighbor, lent them an empty house to use as a publishing headquarters. But on an icy January night the house burned to the ground and took *Guideposts* with it. Everything was gone, including the list of subscribers. The next day Lowell Thomas reported it on his newscast and made a plea for subscribers to send in their names. Another friend, Dewitt Wallace, publisher of the *Reader's Digest* mentioned the plight of *Guideposts* in his magazine. As a result of the fire, *Guideposts* received so much free publicity that their subscription list doubled![5]

Are you beginning to see the universal law of good coming out of bad conditions? I know you may be tempted to say things like, "If I knew Lowell Thomas, I could have good things happen to me too." But you don't need to know Lowell Thomas, Thomas Edison, or Edison Addison (I made the last one up!). You need only to know the author of your existence.

God's method is so unique. Every other advisor steers you away from agony, but he uses your struggle to energize you. You no longer need to view hurt as your enemy, but as your energy. With this view, you can understand the backward things Jesus said like, "Blessed are the poor in spirit" and "Blessed are those who mourn." He converts the terrible into personal advantage.

You no longer need to view hurt as your enemy, but as your energy.

The truth is: fires rage; wars massacre; parents abandon; mates argue; thieves steal; economies bankrupt; businesses bust; skills fade; tumors grow; people die. Another truth is: something blessed is buried in the center of every one of those crises.

Pain has a way of blessing the future. The puncture of the dentist's syringe hurts for the moment, but spares the patient enormous pain later. The result is healthier teeth.

The pit of Joseph in Genesis led to unbelievable hope and success. His brothers sold him into slavery only to meet him years later as a great Egyptian leader.

> Then Joseph said to his brothers, "Please come closer to me." And they came closer. And he said, "I am your brother Joseph, whom you sold into Egypt. And now do not be grieved or angry with yourselves, because you sold me here; for God sent me before you to preserve

life. . . . Now, therefore, it was not you who sent me here, but God; and He has made me a father to Pharaoh and lord of all his household and ruler over all the land of Egypt." (Genesis 45:4–8)

No. Things didn't look too good when he was in the pit. Yes. God was able to transform the darkness into marvelous light and joy. Trust him. If not him, then whom?

♦

God's Prescription for Pain

Be still and know that I am God.

—Psalm 46:10 NIV

♦

SEVEN

BE STILL AND KNOW

One of the deepest frustrations of tragedy is that we feel so helpless. We want to *do* something, to somehow gain some control over the situation. The things we so desperately want seem totally out of reach. We long for

control . . .
 hope . . .
  ability to cope . . .
   progress . . .
    and healing . . .

I am here to tell you that you can have all of these and that there are steps you can take to gain control in your life. However, I must forewarn you—the steps that I suggest may seem insignificant and nonsensical; but they are what God prescribes, and they *will* bring you what you desire: control, hope, the ability to cope, progress, and healing.

There is a story in the Old Testament in the book of 2 Kings that I think you will identify with. The story is about a man named Naaman who was a powerful and respected commander in the army of the king of Aram. But Naaman experienced a devastating tragedy in his life: he was diagnosed with leprosy—a dreaded disease for which there was no cure. Through an Israelite servant girl, Naaman learned of the prophet Elisha who had the power from God to heal him of his leprosy. Naaman did not feel as helpless now. He could take *action*. He traveled a long distance to find Elisha, and he brought with him silver and gold and fine clothing to offer in payment for his healing. But when he came to Elisha's house and made his request known, Elisha, instead of coming out himself and making a fuss over this powerful man, sent his servant with a ridiculous remedy: "Go and wash in the Jordan seven times, and your flesh shall be restored to you and you shall be clean" (2 Kings 5:10).

Naaman was furious.

> "Behold, I thought, He will surely come out to me, and stand and call on the name of the LORD his God, and wave his hand over the place, and cure the leper." . . .

90

Then his servants came near and spoke to him and said, "My father, had the prophet told you to do some great thing, would you not have done it? How much more then, when he says to you, 'Wash and be clean'?" So he went down and dipped himself seven times in the Jordan, according to the word of the man of God; and his flesh was restored like the flesh of a little child, and he was clean. (2 Kings 5:11–14)

In spite of all of Naaman's efforts and expectations, his sole contribution to his healing was to obey a simple, nonsensical command. And to top it all off, when Naaman offered Elisha payment for his services, Elisha would have none of it.

In this section, I will tell you what you can *do* to remedy your pain. But beware: God's prescription for your pain may not be what you expect. Make sure that you are not like Naaman; do not refuse to follow God's prescription because it is not "some great thing."

I think you will discover that the five prescriptions *(Rx)* and desired *Results* outlined in this and the next chapter are exactly what you are after. May God bless you as you seek to follow his prescriptions.

Rx #1: Stand Still
Result #1: Control

If you desire to gain control of the situation that has devasted you, God's first instruction is that you *stand still.*

Be still before the LORD and wait patiently for him. (Psalm 37:7a NIV)

Be still, and know that I am God. (Psalm 46:10 NIV)

"What!" you demand. "My means of gaining control is to be *still!?*" God's whispered answer comes. Be *dependent.* "Yes, but . . ." *Be still . . . and be dependent.* Then weeks later . . . "What can I do to make things better?" *Be dependent.* "Yes, but . . ." *Be still . . . and be dependent.* Then years later . . . "I just don't know what God wants me to do." *Be still. Be dependent. Be still.* "Oh."

It's not unusual to want to *do* something to get your recovery process rolling. But the only thing that will work for now is to wait. Invisible, spiritual moves are being made. Your life is being reordered, though you may not think so. Your role is essential— be still and wait.

The psalmist wrote in the fortieth one,

> I waited patiently for the LORD; and He inclined to me, and heard my cry. He brought me up out of the pit of destruction, out of the miry clay; and He set my feet upon a rock making my footsteps firm. And He put a new song in my mouth, a song of praise to our God; many will see and fear, and will trust in the LORD. How blessed is the man who has made the LORD his trust.

Learn to be still. Just be still. Don't call a friend to complain. Don't write a letter of contempt. Learn to be still. It is so difficult to hear while you are talking.

I see so many who want help, deserve help, and should receive help who don't get help. One reason is they have their own agenda. Then they want friends, foes, and even God to fit their horribly shaky recovery plan. Usual result? No recovery.

Remember the passage quoted earlier in chapter 3: "Incline your ear and come to Me. Listen, that you may live" (Isaiah 55:3). It is our nature to keep talking, keep asking, keep questioning, keep blaming, keep "only if-ing" with such constant chatter that we fail to . . . listen.

The disruption in your life is most likely a whole lot bigger than you are. That is precisely why it is overwhelming. You may have hoped you would be doing better by now, and you just aren't. I continue to remind you to wait . . . wait for God. Be patient with yourself and with him. But do position yourself for his blessings and his prompting by making good decisions. God will make a way.

Rx #2: Trust
Result #2: Hope

God's second prescription for you is that you *trust* him.

> Trust in Him at all times, O people; pour out your heart before Him; God is a refuge for us. (Psalm 62:8)

Once again, what God asks you to do seems to involve no action at all. Your first reaction may be to protest against this "simple" requirement. But anyone who has finally yielded knows that this "simple" job is not simple at all and that only in trusting God do we ultimately find hope.

Why is it so difficult for us to be dependent? Because basically, we are an independent sort. Self-sufficiency is a mark of strength by society's standard. But try calling on society for help in the emergency room or at the cemetery plot.

When I lost my three loved ones, my world was most definitely in shock. I think I eventually began using rental tears, for I surely used all of my own. I was forced to face facts that I could not rearrange. I had to depend on God to make a way because I certainly couldn't.

As long as you insist that you can handle life on your own, you will never find the hope and peace you seek. Pride will keep you independent, self-reliant, and fighting the elements. But dependence will transform your pain into the fuel of hope. Rather than being a source of depression, your pain can ignite your fire for life.

Yes, this idea of total dependence on another is difficult for some to consider. Others, however, are so exhausted from striving that they'll likely be more open to the idea. What I am telling you is not natural to hear. Like Naaman, you must learn that real help comes from a higher plane; and it may not seem right . . . at first.

THE TREASURE AT THE END OF YOURSELF

The way you discover the treasure of hope is to finally come to the end of yourself. Your cures, your desires, your way of thinking must surrender to the Lord's way.

Oswald Chambers wrote in *The Love of God.*

> God is allowing us to prove to the hilt that it cannot be done in any other way than Jesus Christ said; that is by a personal relationship to God through Jesus Christ who is *God and Man—One.* When sooner or later we come to the end of our tether, we hear Jesus Christ say; "Blessed are the poor in spirit" (Matthew 5:3).[1]

We are often tempted to ask God to conquer on our terms, but we must yield instead. The prescription God offers will not necessarily be what you had in mind, but you can be sure that it will be better than what you would calculate. You must let him do victory the way he does it best. And he does win . . . and you will win in him . . . without failure.

When you feel dissatisfied with God's redirection of your life, the following words by Lynn Anderson, in his book, *Finding the Heart to Go On,* may help.

> Our landscapes are littered with broken, bitter people who are angry with God—and everyone else, too—because their dreams were shattered. . . . Why should one ever be bitter about redirection when God is the one who chooses the new direction? Does God make bad choices? Isn't God smart enough to know the best use of my life?[2]

Anderson's last sentence is the question you must ask yourself: "Isn't God smart enough to know the best use of my life?" If you believe he is, trust him.

Bob Grigg, a minister friend in St. Louis, tells of a daddy who had promised his son a reward for being good. The little boy no sooner entered the department store than he saw a truck. "Daddy, this is exactly what I want!" His father told him that he didn't think the truck was really what he wanted. With reluctance, the boy moved on with Dad. "Wow! Daddy, this is what I want! This is it! This soccer ball is all I want! I promise, Dad. This is all I want!"

Once again, Dad rejected his urgent appeal. The little boy sobbed. "What kind of fun is this? Everything I want, I can't have." While the lad was bemoaning his demise, his father said, "Look, son. This is what I want to give you." It was a new, shiny bicycle! The boy could hardly believe it.

Moments earlier he had been pretty peeved with Dad for not giving him the smaller gifts. But the father had something bigger in mind. This is the way your heavenly Father gives gifts to you. You may be arguing with him while he is trying to get you on down the aisle of life to give you the bigger blessing.

HOPE IS IMPEDED BY WORRY

In Matthew 6, Jesus uses logical reasoning to encourage us to relax. He knows you struggle. Hear his words:

> Do not be anxious for your life, as to what you shall eat, or what you shall drink; nor for your body, as to what you shall put on. Is not life more than food, and the body than clothing? Look at the birds of the air, that they do not sow, neither do they reap, nor gather into

barns, and yet your heavenly Father feeds
them. Are you not worth much more than
they? (vv. 25–26)

Think. Consider the facts. Do birds work at fac-
tories or receive paychecks? Something behind the
scene provides for them. He does . . . the Creator of
birdkind . . . and of mankind. God makes a way for
them and for you.

> And which of you by being anxious can add a
> single cubit to his life's span? And why are you
> anxious about clothing? Observe how the lilies
> of the field grow; they do not toil nor do they
> spin, yet I say to you that even Solomon in all
> his glory did not clothe him like one of these.
> But if God so arrays the grass of the field,
> which is alive today and tomorrow is thrown
> into the furnace, will He not much more do so
> for you, O men of little faith? (vv. 27–30)

Men of what? Little amount of that which helps
us see past the surface intimidation and destruction.

> Do not be anxious then, saying, "What shall
> we eat?" or "What shall we drink?" or "With
> what shall we clothe ourselves?" For all these
> things the Gentiles eagerly seek; for your heav-
> enly Father knows that you need all these
> things. But seek first His kingdom and His
> righteousness; and all these things shall be
> added to you. Therefore do not be anxious for
> tomorrow; for tomorrow will care for itself.
> Each day has enough trouble of its own (vv.
> 31–34).

For you who desire definite help? Practice not worrying. Practice trusting him who has work going on in the invisible foundations.

Do not get discouraged with your experiences during your trouble. You will want to take control by manipulating life to your specification. And it won't work. More frustration will set in. But don't give up on yourself or on others who stand by you. Hopefully, you will get the picture that this is bigger than you. Your only hope is to rely on the one bigger than the tragedy . . . the Lord.

The greatest prescription to winning over worry is found in Philippians 4:4–8, and it *works:*

> Rejoice in the Lord always; again I will say, rejoice! Let your forbearing spirit be known to all men. The Lord is near. Be anxious for nothing, but in everything by prayer and supplication with thanksgiving let your requests be made known to God.

We can afford to trust him. His advise is like no other. That, in itself, ought to clue us in.

Faith is waiting on God
  to provide in quiet confidence,
  something that every living creature fathoms
  except man, who must learn it.

—Michael Wells

♦

E I G H T

LOOK
HEAVENWARD

~~~~~~~

Rx #3: Praise and Thanksgiving
Result #3: Ability to Cope

> My tears have been my food day and night. . . .
> I will yet praise him, my Savior and my God.
> (Psalm 42:3a, 5b NIV)

Have you ever felt as engulfed by tears as this
psalm writer felt? I know you have. Our prescription

101

is the same as his—*praise.* When tragedy strikes and your feet are knocked out from under you, you need the strength to somehow get up and make it through the minutes and hours of your days. God's way surprises us once again, for *praise* is the force that helps you cope and helps move you through your days.

This is one of the toughest lessons to accept in all of the Bible. How dare I suggest, with all you have encountered, that praise to God is in order? Thank him for this divorce, this death, this sorrow? As contradictory as it may seem, praise and thanksgiving are two of the most powerful weapons you can wield against pain. This lesson was predominant among all the lessons I learned through my grief. I discovered it in the biblical story of Paul and Silas. Read in Acts 16 about how they were able to cope by praising God in the midst of the ultra depressing confinement of a lonely prison cell.

> # As contradictory as it may seem, praise and thanksgiving are two of the most powerful weapons you can wield against pain.

And the crowd rose up together against them, and the chief magistrates tore their robes off them, and proceeded to order them to be beat-

en with rods. And when they had inflicted
many blows upon them, they threw them into
prison, commanding the jailer to guard them
securely; and he, having received such a command, threw them into the inner prison, and
fastened their feet in the stocks. (vv. 22–24)

How do you think God's prescription of praise
went over with Paul and Silas? Watch what they did.
In turn, watch what God did.

> But about midnight Paul and Silas were pray-
> ing and singing hymns of praise to God, and
> the prisoners were listening to them; and sud-
> denly there came a great earthquake, so that
> the foundations of the prison house were shak-
> en; and immediately all the doors were opened,
> and everyone's chains were unfastened. (vv.
> 25–26)

When you praise God, you too will eventually experience the "and suddenly" that enables you to cope
and leads to your newfound freedom.

Paul and Silas received the rescue that all who are
in pain seek. Chains were unfastened. Doors flew
open. Chains fell. But few allow this wonder to work
in their lives. I believe the Lord has earthquakes
available to shake your grief loose. Praise him that
you will recover. Does Paul sound as if he agrees? Sitting in the potentially ruinous conditions of incar-
ceration, he cheers us,

> Be anxious for nothing, but in prayer and sup-
> plication with thanksgiving let your requests be
> made know to God. (Philippians 4:6)

Learn to praise God because the Bible says to, even when you can't fathom why. Thank him in prayer rather than demand an explanation as to why this is happening.

When Wendy's fiance was murdered, I wanted to take charge and do something that would make her load lighter. But I was bankrupt of all strength and creativity. I could do nothing to make it all go away. I couldn't change the mess that had buried us. Simple thanks to the Lord was all that carried any weight.

Look heavenward. God is to be thanked . . . now. You'll find that praise will buoy you up with the strength you need to cope.

Rx #4: Focus on the Invisible
Result #4: Progress

In order to find rest from your pain, you must look heavenward: take your eyes off your pain and focus them on the invisible hope that lies in realms unseen. This upward and outward focus will pull you along your path and give impetus to your progress.

FOCUS ON THE FUTURE

How do you focus on the invisible? Believe in the future. Believe that you will be victorious even when you see no signs of victory. Believe people will change. Believe things will get better. Believe you will grow stronger. Believe God will bless. Frightening circumstances are great deceivers. Take your eyes

off the current horror and look up to future blessings.

Believers are becomers! You never have to accept
the status quo. Never! You carry invisible hammers,
drills, saws, and nails. By faith, you can dismantle
and construct. You can defy the visible maps that
would guide you into further despair.

Take your eyes off the current horror and look up to future blessings.

Believers are dreamers, and dreamers see what isn't
seen . . . yet. Look into the future. How do you want
it to be? Start seeing it today. "Imaging" is a powerful positive-thinking technique you can use to see a
positive future. Imaging is looking into the future
and seeing yourself in the very setting you desire. If
your goal is to be the top salesman of the year, you
would see yourself taking the steps to achieve that
goal, such as making that winning sales pitch, and
then see yourself getting that award and increase in
salary. I employed this technique before and during
the writing of the book you are now reading.

Before I wrote this book, I told people I was going
to write it. As I work on it now, I tell them that it will
help many in distress. I pray believing that words
from these pages will heal the hearts of men and
women everywhere. But as I work on my word
processor today, only faith says this manuscript will

become a book . . . and it is so! What I believe about this book is fact . . . in the future . . . now!

When Joseph was in the pit, he had no way of knowing God's great plans for him. Yet, what grand plans God had! We must learn to look beyond the seen. We must adjust our vision and look up. Inventory of the present can sink our ship. We can look elsewhere, though, and find hope now.

> Therefore we do not lose heart, but though our outer man is decaying, yet our inner man is being renewed day by day. For momentary, light affliction is producing for us an eternal weight of glory far beyond all comparison, while we look not at the things which are seen, but at the things which are not seen; for the things which are seen are temporal, but the things which are not seen are eternal. (2 Corinthians 4:16–18)

The current state of things is never permanent. Never! Not only do you have the freedom to dream again, you have the responsibility to dream again. Look right into the eye of negativism . . . and stare it down.

Victor Frankl was a concentration camp survivor. He was a successful Viennese psychiatrist before the Nazis threw him into the camp. In a speech he said,

> There is only one reason why I am here today. What kept me alive was you. Others gave up hope. I dreamed. I dreamed that someday I would be here, telling you how I, Victor Frankl, had survived the Nazi concentration camps. I've never been here before, I've never seen any

of you before, I've never given this speech before. But in my dreams, in my dreams, I have stood before you and said these words a thousand times.[1]

Look

I now pass the torch to you. Dare to dream! Your hazard isn't waste. It is opportunity to create a golf course!

Heavenward

FOCUS ON WHAT IS RIGHT ABOUT THE PRESENT

Not surprisingly, Norman Vincent Peale encourages us to focus on the positive:

♦

> A positive thinker is a tough, rugged person, who sees every difficulty and faces all facts realistically. But he is not licked by what he sees. He practices the philosophy of optimism which holds that the good in life outbalances the evil thereof, and he believes that in every difficulty there is inherent good which he intends to find. . . . He does not ignore these realities, but he does not choose to focus on them in such a way that they eclipse the rest of life. . . . Don't depreciate life by enumerating all the things that are wrong with it. Things are wrong, and something has to be done about them. But focus mentally upon all that is right about life; life is good, a lot better than not having it, I should think. A lifetime on this earth doesn't last very long, either. It is here today and gone tomorrow. So love it while you can, and be full of enthusiasm.[2]

Peale is not suggesting that you ignore reality, but that you focus on the solid "appreciatives" of life.

This is not simply good advice or unproven theory. I know that you need hard-hitting information; I know that you can't afford for anyone to "experiment" with your emotions. But this works! Focusing on what is right about the present allows the Creator to take your heart and reenergize it.

I think it was Dr. James Dobson who told of the woman in Florida who was raped, shot in the face, and left for dead. The bullet did not kill her, but it shattered her chin and permanently blinded her.

She was later asked if she had great animosity and hatred toward the assailant. She emphatically responded, "No, not at all. I don't even think about him. That man took a great toll on my life. I choose not to give him one more second by wasting my time thinking about him. Life is too precious."

Indeed, it is.

FOCUS ON THE GOOD

Concentrate on the good. Fill your mind with thoughts of victory, for it surely is everywhere you turn. Think about the "behind the scenes" elements that are working in your favor even when you don't know it.

> Finally, brethren, whatever is true, whatever is honorable, whatever is right, whatever is pure, whatever is lovely, whatever is of good repute, if there is any excellence and if anything worthy of praise, let your mind dwell on these things. (Philippians 4:8)

You will *never, never, never* find better advice. Be of joy. Don't be nervous about anything. Thank

God. Then, think about everything good that you can. Fill your mind with true, honorable, lovely, excellent things. A peace will come over you, and you will not be able to detect how it got there.

FOCUS ON YOUR ULTIMATE VICTORY IN CHRIST

Fix your eyes on Jesus (Hebrews 12:2). This simple instruction from Hebrews speaks volumes. Jesus is the answer. The final victory is found in him alone. The solution is not in a plan, but in the person Jesus. There is no other answer. None. Period. The empty grave is not an empty myth. It is verification that he conquered the ultimate rip in life. If he can conquer the tomb, he can conquer the tumor.

♦

I don't mean to mislead you with the last statement. I do not mean to say that everyone who has a tumor can expect to be healed. The conquering to which I refer is the ultimate and final conclusion . . . beating the grave that illness designs. "In all these things we overwhelmingly conquer through Him who loved us" (Romans 8:37).

Rx #5: Act on the Pain
Result #5: Healing

This last instruction may seem particularly strange. But if you will recall what we discussed in chapters 5 and 6, you can take what we learned there about the blessings and lessons of pain one step further. As you read the two following stories, you will begin to see the energy hidden in your puzzle. Grasp the concept that your threat can be transformed into fuel. With this view, you can understand the backward things Jesus said like, "Blessed are the poor in spirit" and "Blessed are those who mourn." He converts the terrible into personal advantage.

It was Christmas season 1992. I exited a shop as I was headed to lunch. A chubby-fisted, nine-year-old boy with a burr haircut stood on the sidewalk, awaiting his next victim. I was it. "Mister. Would you like some mistletoe for a dollar?" was his pitch as he held a small amount of the greenery wrapped in cellophane.

With clear disgust at him for trying to milk the public for another dollar, I jeered, "Nooo!" Without missing a step in my cadence, I marched myself right on over to the hamburger joint. Hiding behind a partition was this boy's mamma with a box full of individually wrapped mistletoe. She was all smiles.

I was all disgust! She was keeping this boy out of school, exploiting him to help her—probably with her drug habit. Did she have no conscience?

I sat in the cafe, warm and thanking God I wasn't like the likes of her and them. As I dabbed my fries in the catsup, I began to ponder the scenario. I was so bothered by their rudeness . . .

. . . and then I thought again. I began to consider how Jesus would have reacted if he had been in my shoes. In no time at all, I knew it was me who was poor and rude and a fool. I didn't finish my meal. Rather, I headed out with a plan.

There he was. He was still calling out to any who would give him an ear. And . . . no one would. I walked in his direction as if I were passing by with no special awareness of him. He had obviously forgotten

110

my rejection of him twenty minutes earlier. "Mister. Would you want some mistletoe for a dollar?" he reeled.

With great enthusiasm I said, "I don't believe this! I was just needing some mistletoe! But, I am afraid I am going to need ten."

"Ten!" he screamed. "Wait a minute. Wait a minute. That's . . . that's ten dollars! Wow!!" And he ran down the sidewalk, leaped into the air, did a triple axle, and ran back. "Ten dollars!"

He counted out the ten packets, and I counted out the ten dollars. I asked him, "Do you know who Jesus is?"

He nodded that he did. His mother supported his response with, "He does. He learns about him in Bible school."

I said, "Well, I just want you to remember that he is the reason I need this mistletoe today," and I walked off into the parking lot.

Thirty seconds later all could hear this charged voice calling out, "Mi-i-ster! Mi-i-ster!" He ran toward me as fast as his chubby little legs would move, his arm was outstretched. "Mister. Here. I want you to have this." He opened his hand to reveal a dime.

I responded in quietness, "Oh. I don't believe this. I was just now needing a dime. Thank you for giving me this." He beamed, made an about face and skipped all the way back to the sidewalk to encounter more success.

Only minutes earlier, this boy was a blithering nuisance to me. He was a pain—a real problem. But when I took action on the pain, ten dollars bought

111

me a million-dollar attitude. That little boy still blesses my life.

Affirmative action can reverse any difficulty and turn it into treasurable wonder. Initially, I had that setting sized up and figured out: she was using him, and he was an obstruction to an otherwise nice day. Wrong. I was wrong. What I perceived to be irritating was, in reality, opportunity to personally gain unfathomable encouragement. And to think, I nearly threw it all away because he was inconvenient to me.

This event was one of minor irritation. In no way do I mean to compare it to serious tragedy. But the principle is the same whether the pain is minor irritation or overwhelming ordeal. The following account demonstrates how the principle works in severe circumstances.

David P. Jacobsen, an American hostage in Beirut, Lebanon, during the 1980s, learned how to take action on pain. For eighteen months, David endured a harsh existence of chains and blindfolds, of cold dirt floors and terrible loneliness. Listen to the man who was released into the sunlight on November 2, 1986. He came out strengthened by his imprisonment.

> I was snatched off the streets of Beirut on a beautiful May morning in 1985. At the time, I was the head administrator of the largest hospital in Lebanon, and had assumed I was not a likely target for extremists due to the desperate need for medical care in the battle-torn city. I was wrong to think anyone was safe.
>
> I didn't see the men. They threw me into a waiting van and shoved me into a special compartment under the floor of the back seat while

quickly knotting around my head a coarse blindfold and a tight gag. My first reaction was utter terror. I waited for the bullet. But then, in the midst of this nightmare, an astonishing inner calmness took over. "If they are going to shoot you, they wouldn't be bothering with a blindfold."

Calmness is a type of strength. In the following months, I discovered many different strengths—honor, patience, humility, compassion. Most I didn't know I had. If you'd described to me what my captors planned to put me through, I'd have told you that I couldn't have survived the first week. Yet gagged and blindfolded, stripped to my underwear and chained to a wall in a windowless, unheated room, allowed only one watery main meal and one supervised visit to the toilet daily, I was able to survive an ordeal that had been unimaginable to me. In fact, I grew stronger. I had to.

Of all the strengths I discovered in captivity, perhaps forgiveness was the most powerful. When you can forgive those who try to harm you, you lessen the harm they are able to do. You control your victimization. It seems like an impossible thing God asks of us, to forgive those whom we despise. Yet sometimes it is the only way we can rise above our adversity. When I was able to forgive the men who had beaten me, only then was I able to wash the bitter taste from my mouth. When I was able to forgive the men who had held me captive for eighteen months, I was finally able to get on with my life again back home in California. That is why Jesus commands us to forgive our enemies. So that we remain strong.[3]

Jacobsen leaves us with an amazing principle: "You control your victimization." You can learn to control the very event that has victimized you. You can learn to turn the tables on pain and steal its sword. You will not remain handcuffed, blindfolded, and stunned by the dark. Rather, you will arrest it.

You can learn to control the very event that has victimized you.

Do you see how your threat can be transformed into fuel? Do you see how you can view hurt as energy rather than as your enemy? Jacobsen, rather than turning inward with pity and weakness, looked his pain square in the face and acted on it. The threat of his captivity surfaced strengths within him that will bless him for his whole life. You too can gain the upper hand to such an extent that your personal captor will lift you to greater heights.

Victory

Sometimes
    our fate resembles
        a fruit tree in winter.
Who would think
    that those branches
            would turn green again
and blossom,
    but we hope it,
        we know it.

—Johann Goethe

♦

ULTIMATE
VICTORY

You may win your immediate battle, or you may lose. But in Jesus, the apparent loss turns out to be temporary. The final word is that he conquers. How can this be true? Because he succeeded with this truth in the toughest test of all . . . death!

Therefore, I pass along the torch of hope. God will make a way. Your heart can be rebuilt. Victory is near.

Interference can be rude, devastating, and profoundly disruptive. But life will do more than go on;

it will be worth living. I pass along this true story to give you hope.

In and out of trouble as a boy, George seemed to have no direction. He had no plans to be an actor, but the producers who discovered him felt he had a natural talent. Somewhere buried beneath all that toughness, there was a freewheeling style . . . a beguiling nonchalance that attracted people to him. This convinced the box-office barons that he would be a star.

George's first film was completed in record time. All were certain they had found a true star. George received a $25,000 check for his first job. That was a lot of money back then.

Rather than depositing his check right away, George carried it with him and proudly displayed it to all his friends—those five figures symbolized his first success as an actor.

Months passed. All too suddenly, the honeymoon came to an end. The picture failed at the box-office. The producers were bankrupt. When he finally took his check to the bank, it bounced.

He had been pegged a star. Now he was washed up. Yet, this failure turned to his advantage as it ignited a flame for the future. It forced George to dream. He believed that he would be successful.

George Herman's temporary "stardom" hadn't diminished the toughness of his youth; and that rugged, blunt-faced determination is summed up in the nickname that the entire world knows him by today . . . Babe Ruth.[1]

Recovery Begins with a Spark

You, my friend, have the spark of victory buried deep inside of you. Given opportunity, that spark will be fanned into flame by hope, faith, and love.

Do you believe that because you can't eat now that you will never eat again? You will. Do you think that because you cannot focus at work, that you will never put in another good day? You will.

Dennis Byrd was a pro defensive lineman for the New York Jets. One day, as he pursued the quarterback for a sack, he collided with his teammate. The crash was terrible. He recalls the scary moments when he lay on his back and stared through his helmet at the gray sky.

> Kyle Clifton, our middle linebacker, was the first to come over. "Let's go, buddy," he said, expecting me to just jump to my feet. "Get up. Let's go."
>
> "Kyle," I said, "I can't. I'm paralyzed."
>
> His face turned pale, almost blank. It was as if everything that meant anything to him had drained from his body in that instant. It was in his eyes, such a lonely look, like he was the only man left on earth. He realized I was lying there powerless, paralyzed, and he didn't know how to deal with it. He couldn't say a word. There was nothing to say.
>
> Then Marvin kneeled by my side. Marvin Washington, my roommate and closest friend.
>
> "Dennis," he said softly, "what's the matter?"
>
> "I don't have any feeling in my legs, Marvin," I said. "I can't feel my legs."

He lowered his voice, almost to a whisper. "Just try, baby," he hissed. "Try."[2]

This is where it begins with you. *Just try.* You may feel you cannot take another breath or another step or another day. But there is within you the spark that is needed to get the fire going. *Just try.*

Dennis Byrd fanned that spark into flame and made vast improvements through regular therapy and relentless determination. What was true of Dennis Byrd is true of you. There is a spark of energy rallying for your cause . . . within you.

In the following poem by Virgil Fry —*A Prayer of One Experiencing Loss*—I think you will see your pain and your struggle . . . and your hope.

Lord God,
    Giver of life
    Source of all that exists
Hear my prayer of pain.

My life is in shambles
The one I love dearly is gone.
Removed from my world
Yanked from my heart.

Often I wonder, Lord
    Am I crazy?
    Am I selfish?
    Am I unfaithful?

Often I question, Lord
    Are you aware?
    Are you responsible?
    Are you there?

120

Yet, in the midst of dark moments
Flickers of renewed energy spark my soul.
Memories that bring tears sometimes bring
    unexpected smiles.

My broken heart remembers:
    You are not a distant god but rather,
    you are God—revealed as One
        acquainted with grief.

Lord, I beg for your assured presence.
For those who
    share my grief
    And allow me to be me,
    I thank you.
For having my heart touched
    by the love of the one now gone,
    I thank you.

♦

May your gentle arms of comfort
    soothe my aching spirit.
May your name—I AM—
    be victoriously proclaimed,
    even in the valley of death.

"In the midst of dark moments flickers of renewed energy spark [your] soul" as well as Dr. Fry's.
You may feel that there is no life left in your soul, but
you can be certain that there is, and that God knows
where it is.

Although you cannot feel it, the energy is there. It
is odorless. It is in remission. But believe it . . . it is
there. Your devastation has smothered all awareness
of any ambition and drive, but the spark is there.
Not only is it buried deep within you, but the Lord

will fan it until it bursts forth into a strong flame. God is working on your spark.

Although you may feel very lonely, you are not alone. Though you may detect nothing good in your life, good is there. A spark of energy is being fanned by the Master Candlemaker. You will make it. You are going to be okay.

Don't get to thinking that this good can never happen to you. You are not the lone exception to the "spark" rule. Just as you have discovered that you are not immune to catastrophe, know that you are not immune to the spark. You are a victim of tragedy, but know that you are also a victim of good. Be prepared. You are about to *flare up!*

Just as you have discovered that you are not immune to catastrophe, know that you are not immune to the spark.

Peace That Passes Comprehension

> And the peace of God, which surpasses all comprehension, shall guard your hearts and your minds in Christ Jesus. (Philippians 4:7)

What is this peace that "surpasses all comprehension?" How will you know you have it if you can't comprehend it? We know that God manufactures peace—we surely can't. The part we can't comprehend is how we get it. While we can't comprehend how we get it, we know we have it by the way we feel.

Cliff and Wanda Leppanen lost their married daughter, Susan, to a bacterial virus at Thanksgiving, 1992. Regarding the above passage, Wanda says,

> I took the Bible—the one that belonged to Susan—and I read Philippians 4:6 out loud over and over. I said, "Peace, Lord, where is that peace that passes all understanding you have promised?" Suddenly—almost magically—a calmness flowed through me. It felt so wonderful to breath deeply again that I smiled and said thank you, thank you Lord. . . . And that peace, my friends, is the difference between leading a productive life and taking sleeping pills, a mental institution or suicide.

Peace is part of your victory. And, how does this peace "guard your hearts and minds in Christ Jesus"? God's peace keeps you from going crazy—from losing it—when you are certain you will.

When the deaths of my three loved ones rocked my life, I found myself struggling for control. But I found that the more I gave up that which I could not change anyway, the more he gave peace and comfort to me. What was it that I gave up? I surrendered the need to harp about the negatives that weren't going to change.

You may be so devastated that you can hardly function, but his peace will invisibly keep your heart and mind together.

Ultimate
Victory

♦

Victory Is in God Alone

Our educated society prides itself in being open-minded. But I see two major problems with our "open-mindedness." First, our society's mind is not so open when it comes to the concept of Jesus, the Lamb of God. Second, as the worship of God is pushed aside, the rate of crime, pain, and damage appear to proportionately increase. Open-mindedness with respect to the opinions of others is one thing, but to relegate Jehovah God to the status of personal opinon goes way beyond open-mindedness. Does it not seem right that in order to reduce pain, society needs to restore its spiritual conviction?

Think about it: Is our society on course for destruction or life? Things are not getting better. I don't mean to be an alarmist, but I do mean to point out what we all know. Our streets are increasingly dangerous, and even our locked houses are not entirely safe. Respect for authority is antiquity. We must wake up to the truth that our world is feeding from the gutter.

Can we not see that prayer disallowed in public schools is simultaneous with the dilemma of "What shall we do with all this prison overload?" Somehow it needs to register that the two connect.

Many who set themselves up as leaders and problem solvers are often derailed themselves. To make matters worse, television's religious programs are often filled with empty words, makeup, and pitches for money.

In *Passion for Jesus,* Mike Bickle addresses the distorted view of God that many "believers" hold:

The downward spiral of morality in our society is directly proportional to the loss of our understanding of the greatness of God. In the minds of most people who believe there is a God, He is little more than an elected official—not to be taken too seriously.

Why does our society have such a limited and irreverent view of God? The answer is simple. The church has not proclaimed it! The church's concept of God is too small.

For many Christians Jesus is more like Santa Claus or a pop psychologist than the holy Other who will judge heaven and earth by His word.[3]

The unbelieving that goes on within the Christian circle is astounding.

The unbelieving that goes on within the Christian circle is astounding. Have we become so independently wise that the true God has been reduced to one of many sources of guidance? Has the Lord taken a backseat to philosophy, myth, and the daily horoscope? It is time to reevaluate our enthusiasm for the Lord. Only God can straighten out this sick swirl of ours.

There is hope! But it is not in the "me" style of "doing my own thing." In my observation, this mentality controls every generation today—not just the younger one. If we are serious about putting broken hearts together again, we must acknowledge the mystery of the Lord's presence and his provisionary desires.

The ancient passage from the book of Matthew has vital application today:

> Enter by the narrow gate; for the gate is wide, and the way is broad that leads to destruction, and many are those who enter by it. For the gate is small, and the way is narrow that leads to life, and few are those who find it. (Matthew 7:13, 14)

But the narrow way is not what you might think. It is not narrow-mindedness. The typical narrow-minded shouters from church pulpits and pews who squint their eyes and snarl at our stupidity are not on the "narrow way" Matthew speaks of. The narrow way is on track with the Creator, Maintainer, and Sustainer . . . the Lord God.

Our broken world is filled with pain and cries out for healing. Efforts to provide healing are made by lawmakers, philosophers, counselors, and religious shouters, but true victory over pain is found only in the Almighty God and only on the narrow way.

God whispers to us in our pleasures,
speaks in our conscience,
but shouts in our pains:
it is His megaphone
to rouse a deaf world.

—C. S. Lewis

◆

THE FOG
WILL LIFT

The following stories are true. Some of the names have been changed to protect the people involved.

When my husband died in a car accident, leaving me alone at twenty-one to raise eighteen-month-old twin daughters, I thought that my world had fallen apart. In the next few months, I went though a wide range of emotions. I went from being sad, to being scared, even to being angry at him, and finally to acceptance. There were times I felt so alone. I thought I'd never remarry.

Now, eighteen years later, I have a wonderful husband, a son and another daughter. Time and memories helped. When I first remarried, even though I was ready to go on, I still hadn't totally accepted the accident.

I was lucky that I met a very understanding person who let me talk things out when I needed to. It wasn't everyday or even every week or month—but there were times. I finally came to realize that accidents just happen and life goes on.

—Linda McEntee

Linda has hurt where some of you hurt. She hasn't experienced the entire range of struggle. No one has. But she has certainly walked the fires of ripping pain. The story of Linda McEntee has been told throughout the ages . . . only with different names attached to each varying saga of destruction.

But I want you to know of the survivors and the endurers who encountered horror and incredible pain. Linda McEntee sets the stage for this chapter in order that you can hear from others who were blown away by that which was far too deep to fathom. Maybe this or another story will relate to your fresh encounter.

These have successfully endured the impossible. They are shared with you at the moment to let you know that you will make it. You will be all right. No, you will never be the same, but you will be all right.

I was sorry that my marriage didn't work. However, to this union were born Denise and Michael. Denise is a joy to my heart. Michael is a corker.

Michael was born with several major abnormalities. He had club feet and both were turned up. They touched the inside of each leg. Rather than the urinary tract being completed at the end of the penis, the opening was on the side.

A rare disease, Coloboma, left the nerves missing from the back of the eyes. There is no cure. Many born with this disease remain blind for life. He was also tongue-tied.

I was devastated. I cried every night as I rocked him to sleep.

The doctors clipped his tongue. It took three surgeries to correct his feet. Another surgery repaired his urinary tract. Two churches offered prayers that Michael could see. At three months, I saw Michael follow the red ears on his dog bank on the dresser.

By his third month, we had made tremendous progress. He will always have blind spots in his eyes. His vision is not good, but he has partial vision straight ahead with the right eye and out one side of the left.

At six months we learned that this bundle of blessing was mentally retarded. The devastation started again.

I worked endlessly to get Michael to utter sounds, throw balls, and crawl. He didn't learn to walk until he was three. I always knew he would.

The best advice I received was from the doctors. They told me not to give up my life for him. That to do so would not help Michael. So, I included Michael in everything that we did. We took him everywhere with us and treated him as normal—yet, with physical limitations.

At age fifteen, Michael can now write his name, make our shopping list, count to ten (nine out of ten times!), and do the claps, yells, and turns of line dances. He loves to help with the cooking.

This light of my life is always positive. "Oh well, you'll live." "You be all right." "You no need anyway." "Maybe him need it." Michael gifts others with joy, elation, and laughter at his openness and charm. He always speaks honestly, "You pretty" or "You old!"

When he gets older, I think he will be able to live in a group home. He wants to live in Quincy, Illinois, and ride his bicycle to the dance—"I'll be all right."

—Janet Shelts

I married at nineteen with so many hopes and idealistic thoughts of how marriage should be. Instead, it became the darkest time of my life. Home, a place where we should feel secure and loved, a place that should be a safe shelter, never became that for me. I was an abused wife—physically, verbally, and emotionally.

During those few years that I was married, the feelings of hopelessness and despair increased. Eventually, all my husband had to do was walk through the front door, and I became sick at my stomach. How much he'd had to drink was always a question. Liquor made him even more violent. My every word was guarded for fear of saying the wrong thing and sending him into a rage.

His constant cursing and belittling whittled away at my self-esteem. I began to believe that what he said about me was true. My house turned into a deep, dark pit. Any light was beyond my reach. It seemed that darkness was swallowing all my dreams and me. The bruises on the outside only deepened the scars on the inside.

The prayerful help and support of my family and close friends enabled me to survive. My toddler son and I crawled together out of the well.

During those terrible years and to this day my favorite Scripture is Romans 5:3–5. As I would read these words, I could feel myself getting stronger. I know that my suffering produced endurance, that my endurance produced character, and that my character produced hope. My hope did not disappoint me, because God's love was poured into my heart through the Holy Spirit that was given to me.

I remained single for ten years. My guardian angel on earth, my sister, introduced me to a very gentle, loving, kind-hearted man. This man is a gift from God. Ten years is a long time to wonder if home normality will ever be restored.

The years of pain produced growth and character in me. I believe that what I endured and learned prepared me and trained me to appreciate the true treasure I have in my husband.

I believe that no matter what comes to pass in your life, it will have its favorable result. God is always with you. You may not know his purpose at the time, but God will be there for you. He was for me.

My prayer for you who suffer in this way is that you will not lose hope, that you will do more than endure, that you will become a stronger person.

—Elise Kirkland
(name changed)

Like a lot of other couples today, we had decided to wait a few years before starting our family. We had things all figured out and knew just how things were going to go. But we didn't know or even consider that God's plans would be different. Our whole situation began with fertility problems.

With God's help, after months of prayer, fasting, and medical testing, Jeania became pregnant with our first child. To say we were thrilled doesn't even begin to express our joy.

We had waited a long time and been through what we thought was a lot of struggle to have this child, so our happiness was even more intense.

Everything was back on course. Our plans were being fulfilled, and God was going to bless us. The first half of the pregnancy went along great, but then without any warning, we found ourselves in the hospital delivery room having our first child. Our son, Remington, was born on January 18, 1991—four months premature. At this age his lungs were not well developed and he survived only a few minutes.

To this day, we still can't express the feelings that losing him brought, and still brings, to our hearts. We were stunned, shocked, and most of all hurt very deeply. Even though we were surrounded by friends and family, we still felt alone. We were so crushed that we didn't even have the emotional energy to pray, but we did have wonderful friends and family who carried us and prayed for us when we couldn't.

After another round of tests, the doctors assured us that this was an "unusual" occurrence and that we should have no further problems with pregnancy. So after more prayers and encouragement from the people close to us, Jeania was pregnant again—this time without having to endure fertility tests and months of waiting. Once again we were excited beyond words. God had blessed us with another child. When we went for our first ultrasound, we were even more thrilled to find that we were having twins. I had always wanted twins, and we were convinced that this was God's very special gift to us. But things were difficult from the start with this pregnancy, and Jeania had to be put to bed early on to avoid going into premature labor.

Before we knew it, we were in the middle of another struggle. After lots of prayers and fasting, we found ourselves in the hospital again, and after a week long ordeal in the hospital, our twins were born prematurely. Megan and Tyler were born August 22, 1991, and survived only a few minutes.

Not only were we devastated by losing our children, but it seemed that our dream to have children had died too. We were angry, very angry. Sometimes with friends, sometimes with God, sometimes with each other, and sometimes just at the whole situation. In a period of only eight months, we had buried our first three children. The feeling is almost impossible to describe . . . our hearts literally ached—physically. The doctors told us there was no way that we could have any more children.

We were so confused. God could have saved our children, but he didn't. We had prayed and fasted, but he still didn't answer our prayers the way we wanted. Now we were faced with the prospect of never having children. We felt that God was trying to tell us something, but we didn't know what. After more prayers, tears, and heartaches, we decided to adopt a baby. Through a series of miraculous happenings, God lead us to our third son, Colton, within two months after the death of our twins. And within another year, he brought us our second daughter, Kirstin. Anyone who knows anything about adoption knows that adoptions working out this quickly is truly miraculous. Our hurting and empty hearts were now full of love and joy. Sometimes we even wonder who else God is going to send us.

Our story has definitely had a happy ending, but we still wonder why God chose to give us our family the way he did. We've prayed and studied a lot on this subject, and we still don't understand why things happened the way they did. In fact, we probably won't ever understand for sure until we get to heaven, but there are some important things we have learned. First of all, we learned that you never completely heal. There are still times when a song on the radio or a particular setting will remind us of the children we lost, and we'll break down and cry again. We are thrilled with the children we have and would not trade them for anything, but they in no way replace the children we have lost. But probably the most important thing we have learned is that God is in control of everything, and any appearance that we are in control of any situation is only an illusion.

—Mike and Jeania Ishmael

For twenty-six years I blocked out a crucial portion of my life. My twelve-year-old brother began sexually abusing me when I was only four. This behavior continued for the next three years. Not until I was thirty-two and listening to Amy Grant's "Is There a God up in the Heavens" did any flashbacks occur.

I thought I was going crazy. The feelings of total disbelief, anger, and guilt consumed me. Then more memories surfaced. I became that scared little girl all over again. I didn't know if I could live through it again. I was physically sick and mentally drained.

The next few months were difficult. Very difficult. I spent time reading materials in search of big answers to tough questions. I talked with survivors. I began to study the Bible and to pray. Psalm 138 and 139 helped me so much.

The Lord has blessed me during these past two years. I finally feel whole; something I never felt before. God is to be glorified as he alone has helped me to gain freedom in my mind.

One unusual blessing occurred when a victim needed my help. I still thank God that he would let me be a survivor in order to help someone else.

—Marta DuQuoin
(name changed)

I do not share these testimonies in an effort to say: "See, you don't really have a problem." Nothing of the sort. These are witnesses for your future. Be comforted. Their message to you? You will make it. They made it!

Linda never had the chance to say goodbye to her first husband. Her heart exploded. Yet, life has gone on with her in it. She not only survived; she is happy again. Janet's lovable boy remains handicapped; yet, his charm merely leads us to see that we are the handicapped ones.

And look at Elise. She didn't know if she'd ever meet a man who would offer security and safety in a home. Ten years of waiting must have seemed hopeless and maybe even useless. Things still tug at Mike and Jeania. Colton and Kirstin are wonderful blessings! But as long as memories exist, Remington and Megan and Tyler are injury to their hearts.

Marta is making the best of it. She is a winner. She does not deny the ugly hurt of her past, but she uses that personal harm to give aid to other victims.

Each of these has been in your shoes. Their message? Don't quit. Don't take the overdose. Don't pull the trigger. Don't give up. These witnesses have specialized in adapting to uninvited circumstances. They have walked down your dark hallway or maybe into your empty bedroom.

Can you walk this tightrope? Can you survive this road of dismay and disbelief? Yes. Linda, Janet, Elise, and the others pass the torch on to you. The fog will lift. Your step will become a little more stable. You, too, will recover.

The Church is cluttered with shipwrecked scholars
who thought the Bible was written for
understanding and did not recognize
it was written to give life.

—Michael Wells

♦

ELEVEN

HEAVEN SENDS ITS LOVE

Heaven sees your pain and hears your cry. Heaven sends its love:

And we know that God causes all things to work together for good to those who love God, to those who are called according to His purpose. (Romans 8:28)

Have I not commanded you? Be strong and courageous! Do not tremble or be dismayed, for the LORD your God is with you wherever you go. (Joshua 1:9)

O foolish men and slow of heart to believe in all that the prophets have spoken! Was it not necessary for

141

the Christ to suffer these things and to enter into His glory? (Luke 24:25, 26)

It is good for me that I was afflicted, that I may learn Thy statutes. (Psalm 119:71)

But Peter arose and ran to the tomb; stooping and looking in, he saw the linen wrappings only; and he went away to his home, marveling at that which had happened. (Luke 24:12)

But Thou, O LORD, art a shield about me, my glory, and the One who lifts my head. I was crying to the LORD with my voice, and He answered me from His holy mountain. I lay down and slept; I awoke, for the LORD sustains me. I will not be afraid of ten thousands of people who have set themselves against me round about. (Psalm 3:3–6)

And hope does not disappoint, because the love of God has been poured out within our hearts through the Holy Spirit who was given to us. (Romans 5:5)

Consider it all joy, my brethren, when you encounter various trials, knowing that the testing of your faith produces endurance. And let endurance have its perfect result, that you may be perfect and complete, lacking in nothing. (James 1:2–4)

Do not be surprised at the fiery ordeal among you, which comes upon you for testing, as though some strange thing were happening to you. (1 Peter 4:12)

I will bless the LORD who has counseled me; indeed, my mind instructs me in the night. I have set the LORD continually before me; because He is at my right hand, I will not be shaken. Therefore my heart is glad, and my glory rejoices; my flesh also will dwell securely. (Psalm 16:7–9)

Heaven

Sends

Its

Love

♦

For this reason I say to you, do not be anxious for your life, as to what you shall eat, or what you shall drink; nor for your body, as to what you shall put on. Is not life more than food, and the body than clothing? (Matthew 6:25)

God . . . who gives life to the dead and calls into being that which does not exist. In hope against hope he believed. (Romans 4:17, 18a)

And such confidence we have through Christ toward God. Not that we are adequate in ourselves to consider anything as coming from ourselves, but our adequacy is from God. (2 Corinthians 3:4, 5)

Remember my affliction and my wandering, the wormwood and bitterness. Surely my soul remembers and is bowed down within me. This I recall to my mind, therefore I have hope. The LORD'S lovingkindnesses indeed never cease, for His compassions never fail. They are new every morning; great is Thy faithfulness. "The LORD is my portion," says my soul, "therefore I have hope in Him." (Lamentations 3:19–24)

O LORD, be gracious to us; we have waited for Thee. Be Thou their strength every morning, our salvation also in the time of distress. (Isaiah 33:2)

Look at the birds of the air, that they do not sow, neither do they reap, nor gather into barns, and yet your heavenly Father feeds them. Are you not worth much more than they? (Matthew 6:26)

I will sing to the LORD as long as I live; I will sing praise to my God while I have my being. Let my meditation be pleasing to Him; as for me, I shall be glad in the LORD. (Psalm 104:33, 34)

Let us hold fast the confession of our hope without wavering, for He who promised is faithful. (Hebrews 10:23)

Christ was faithful as a Son over His house whose house we are, if we hold fast our confidence and the boast of our hope firm until the end. (Hebrews 3:6)

And which of you by being anxious can add a single cubit to his life's span? (Matthew 6:27)

"Do not fear, for those who are with us are more than those who are with them." Then Elisha prayed and said, "O LORD, I pray, open his eyes that he may see." And the LORD opened the servant's eyes, and he saw; and behold, the mountain was full of horses and chariots of fire all around Elisha. (2 Kings 6:16, 17)

I pray that the eyes of your heart may be enlightened, so that you may know what is the hope of His calling, what are the riches of the glory of His inheritance in the saints, and what is the surpassing greatness of His power toward us who believe. (Ephesians 1:18, 19)

And why are you anxious about clothing? Observe how the lilies of the field grow; they do not toil nor do they spin, yet I say to you that even Solomon in all his glory did not clothe himself like one of these. But if God so arrays the grass of the field, which is alive today and tomorrow is thrown into the furnace, will He not much more do so for you, O men of little faith? (Matthew 6:28–30)

God sees not as man sees, for man looks at the outward appearance, but the LORD looks at the heart. (1 Samuel 16:7)

The LORD is my light and my salvation; whom shall I fear? The Lord is the defense of my life; whom shall I dread? When evildoers came upon me to devour my flesh, my adversaries and my enemies, they stumbled and fell. Though a host encamp against me, my heart will not fear; though war arise against me, in spite of this I shall be confident. (Psalm 27:1–3)

Even though I walk through the valley of the shadow of death, I fear no evil; for Thou art with me; Thy rod and Thy staff, they comfort me. (Psalm 23:4)

For God has shut up all in disobedience that He might show mercy to all. Oh, the depth of the riches both of the wisdom and knowledge of God! How unsearchable are His judgments and unfathomable His ways! (Romans 11:32, 33)

Therefore I am well content with weaknesses, with insults, with distresses, with persecutions, with difficulties, for Christ's sake; for when I am weak, then I am strong. (2 Corinthians 12:10)

Do not be anxious then, saying, "What shall we eat?" or "What shall we drink?" or "With what shall we clothe ourselves?" (Matthew 6:31)

For of His fulness we have all received, and grace upon grace. (John 1:16)

Set your mind on the things above, not on the things that are on earth. (Colossians 3:2)

Devote yourselves to prayer, keeping alert in it with an attitude of thanksgiving. (Colossians 4:2)

"For My thoughts are not your thoughts, neither are your ways My ways," declares the LORD. "For as the heavens are higher than the earth, so are My ways higher than your ways, and My thoughts than your thoughts." (Isaiah 55:8, 9)

Do you not know? Have you not heard? The everlasting God, the LORD, the Creator of the ends of the earth does not become weary or tired. His understanding is inscrutable. He gives strength to the weary, and to him who lacks might He increases power. Though youths grow weary and tired, and vigorous young men stumble badly, yet those who wait for the LORD will gain new strength; they will mount up with wings like eagles, they will run and not get tired, they will walk and not become weary. (Isaiah 40:28–31)

Is anything too difficult for the LORD? (Genesis 18:14a)

But Moses said to the people, "Do not fear! Stand by and see the salvation of the LORD which He will accomplish for you today; for the Egyptians whom you have seen today, you will never see them again forever. The LORD will fight for you while you keep silent." Then the LORD said to Moses, "Why are you crying out to Me? Tell the sons of Israel to go forward." (Exodus 14:13–15)

With men this is impossible, but with God all things are possible. (Matthew 19:26)

Now faith is the assurance of things hoped for, the conviction of things not seen. (Hebrews 11:1)

The LORD bless you, and keep you; the LORD make His face shine on you, and be gracious to you; the LORD lift up His countenance on you, and give you peace. (Numbers 6:24–26)

Do not call to mind the former things, or ponder things of the past. Behold, I will do something new, now it will spring forth; will you not be aware of it? I will even make a roadway in the wilderness, rivers in the desert. (Isaiah 43:18, 19)

One thing I do: forgetting what lies behind and reaching forward to what lies ahead, I press on toward the goal for the prize of the upward call of God in Christ Jesus. (Philippians 3:13, 14)

In the wilderness He fed you manna which your fathers did not know, that He might humble you and that He might test you, to do good for you in the end. Otherwise, you may say in your heart, "My power and the strength of my hand made me this wealth." But you shall remember the LORD your God, for it is He who is giving you power to make wealth. (Deuteronomy 8:16–18)

"For I know the plans that I have for you," declares the LORD, "plans for welfare and not for calamity to give you a future and a hope. Then you will call upon Me and come and pray to Me, and I will listen to you. And you will seek Me and find Me, when you search for Me with all your heart. And I will be found by you," declares the LORD, "and I will restore your fortunes and will gather you from all the nations and from all the places where I have driven you," declares the LORD, "and I will bring you back to the place from where I sent you into exile." (Jeremiah 29:11–14)

SUGGESTED
READING

Don't lay this book down and be done. Take affirmative action. You can fan your spark into a fire for life. The following books and video tape will fill your heart and mind with hope:

The Road Less Traveled,
   by M. Scott Peck
In the Eye of the Storm,
   by Max Lucado
Finding the Heart to Go On,
   by Lynn Anderson

Simple Faith,
   by Charles Swindoll

The Holy Spirit Makes No Earthly Sense,
   by Terry Rush

Afraid God Works, Afraid He Doesn't,
   by Terry Rush

When God Whispers Your Name,
   by Max Lucado

Abba's Child,
   by Brennan Manning

High Hope for the Human Heart
   (video cassette), by Terry Rush

   This video contains interviews with people of
fame (Loretta Lynn, Gene Stallings, Curt Flood,
and others) regarding their struggles and disap-
pointments, their avenues of recovery, and the
certainty of God's compassion.

   Order by sending a check for $23.45 (includes
shipping and handling) to: Memorial Drive
church of Christ, 747 S. Memorial Dr., Tulsa, OK
74112. (Also available in opened-captioned for
hearing impaired and the Spanish language.)

   If I can be of help to you, write me in care of the
address above. Let me know of your struggles, pains,
and glimpses of hopes. I will do what I can to help
you as you make progress for the future.

NOTES

CHAPTER ONE. MY STORY

1. *Leadership* 15, Fall 1994, 24.

CHAPTER TWO. SOMEDAY, I WILL BE ME AGAIN

1. Max Lucado, *In the Eye of the Storm* (Dallas: Word Publishing, 1991), 11.
2. Paula D'Arcy, "Song for Sarah," *Guideposts* (Carmel, N.Y.: Guideposts, 1979), 10–120.

CHAPTER THREE. SPIRITUAL ANSWERS FOR SPIRITUAL CREATURES

1. Brennan Manning, *Lion and Lamb* (Waco, Tex.: Chosen Books, 1986), 13, 14.
2. Ibid., 15.
3. Oswald Chambers, *The Love of God* (Grand Rapids, Mich.: Discovery House, 1985), 22, 23.

CHAPTER FOUR. GOD CARES

1. David A. Redding, *Before You Call, I Will Answer* (Old Tappan, N.J.: Fleming H. Revell Co., 1985), 30, 31.

Chapter Five. The Privilege of Pain

1. Dallas Willard, preface to *The Spirit of the Disciplines* (New York: Harper & Row, 1988).
2. C. S. Lewis, *The Problem of Pain* (New York: The Macmillan Co., 1974), 14.
3. Dr. Paul Brand and Philip Yancey, *Pain: The Gift Nobody Wants* (New York: Harper Collins, 1993), 218.
4. Charles Swindoll, *Encourage Me* (Portland: Multnomah Press, 1982), 36.
5. F. B. Meyer, *Elijah* (Ft. Washington, Pa.: Christian Literature Crusade, 1978), 28, 29.
6. Helen Steiner Rice, *"Just for You"* (Garden City, N.Y.: Doubleday & Co., Inc., 1967), 17.
7. Brand and Yancey, *Pain*.
8. Max Lucado, *Tell Me the Secrets* (Wheaton, Ill.: Crossway Books, Good News Publishers, 1993), 25.

Chapter Six. The Lessons of Pain

1. Melody Beattie, *The Lessons of Love* (New York: Harper Collins, 1994), 207–13.
2. Michael Molinos, *The Spiritual Guide* (Auburn, Maine: The Seed Sowers, Christian Books Publishing House, 1982), 28.
3. Martha Snell Nicholson, *Heart Held High* (n.p., n.d.).
4. Brand and Yancey, *Pain,* 218
5. Richard Lewis Detrich, *Norman Vincent Peale* (n.p.: Ideals Publishing Corp., 1969), 57.

Chapter Seven. Be Still and Know

1. Chambers, *Love,* 27.
2. Lynn Anderson, *Finding the Heart to Go On* (San Bernardino, Calif.: Here's Life Publishers, 1991), 115.

CHAPTER EIGHT. LOOK HEAVENWARD

1. Harvey Mackay, *Swim with the Sharks* (New York: Ivy Books, 1988), 73.
2. Detrich, *Peale,* 71.
3. Norman Vincent Peale, *Daily Guideposts 1994* (Carmel, N.Y.: Guideposts Associates, Inc., 1993), 42.

CHAPTER NINE. ULTIMATE VICTORY

1. Paul Aurandt, *Paul Harvey's The Rest of the Story* (Garden City, N.Y.: Doubleday & Co., Inc., 1977), 155, 156.
2. Dennis Byrd, *Rise and Walk* (New York: Harper Collins, n.d.), 2.
3. Mike Bickle, *Passion for Jesus* (Orlando, Fla.: Creation House, 1993), 48.

BIBLIOGRAPHY

Anderson, Lynn. *Finding the Heart to Go On.* San Bernardino, Calif.: Here Life Publishers, 1991.

Aurandt, Paul. *Paul Harvey's The Rest of the Story.* Garden City, N.Y.: Doubleday & Co., 1977.

Beattie, Melody. *The Lessons of Love.* New York: Harper Collins, 1994.

Bickle, Mike. *Passion for Jesus.* Orlando, Fla.: Creation House, 1993.

Brand, Paul, and Philip Yancey. *Pain: The Gift Nobody Wants.* New York: Harper Collins, 1993.

Byrd, Dennis. *Rise and Walk.* New York: Harper Collins, n.d.

Chambers, Oswald. *The Love of God.* Grand Rapids, Mich.: Discovery House, 1985.

D'Arcy, Paula. "Song for Sarah." *Guideposts.* Carmel, N.Y.: Guideposts, 1979.

Detrich, Richard Lewis. *Norman Vincent Peale.* N.p.: Ideals Publishing Corp., 1969.

Lewis, C. S. *The Problem of Pain.* New York: The Macmillan Co., 1974.

Lucado, Max. *In the Eye of the Storm.* Dallas: Word Publishing, 1991.

———. *Tell Me the Secrets.* Wheaton, Ill.: Crossway Books, Good News Publishers, 1993.

♦

————. *When God Whispers Your Name.* Dallas: Word Publishing, 1994.

Mackay, Harvey. *Swim with the Sharks.* New York: Ivy Books, 1988.

Manning, Brennan. *Abba's Child.* Colorado Springs: Nav-Press, 1994.

————. *Lion and Lamb.* Waco, Tex.: Chosen Books, 1986.

Meyer, F. B. *Elijah.* Ft. Washington, Pa.: Christian Literature Crusade, 1978.

Molinos, Michael. *The Spiritual Guide.* Auburn, Maine: The Seed Sowers, Christian Books Publishing House, 1982.

Peale, Norman Vincent. *Daily Guideposts 1994.* Garden City, N.Y.: Guideposts Associates, Inc., 1993.

Peck, M. Scott. *The Road Less Traveled.* New York: Simon & Schuster, Inc., 1978.

Redding, David A. *Before You Call, I Will Answer.* Old Tappan, N.J.: Fleming H. Revell Co., 1985.

Rush, Terry. *Afraid God Works, Afraid He Doesn't.* West Monroe, La.: Howard Publishing Co., Inc., 1991.

————. *The Holy Spirit Makes No Earthly Sense.* West Monroe, La.: Howard Publishing Co., Inc., 1991.

Swindoll, Charles. *Encourage Me.* Portland: Multnomah Press, 1982.

————. *Simple Faith.* Dallas: Word Publishing, 1991.

Willard, Dallas. *The Spirit of the Disciplines.* New York: Harper & Row, 1988.

Printed in the United States
By Bookmasters